The
ELK HUNTER

The
ELK HUNTER

The Ultimate Source Book on Elk and Elk Hunting
from Past to Present, for the Beginner and Expert Alike

By Don Laubach and Mark Henckel
with an introduction by Gordon Eastman

Library of Congress Catalog Card Number: 87-90834
ISBN: 1-931832-65-X

Published by:
Don Laubach
Box 85
Gardiner, MT 59030

Distributed by:
Riverbend Publishing
P.O. Box 5833
Helena, MT 59604
1-866-787-2363

Cover and illustrations by John Potter

Dedication

This book is dedicated
to elk hunting widows everywhere
(especially Dee Laubach and Carol Henckel)
who keep the home fires burning
while elk hunters have all the fun.

TABLE OF CONTENTS

ACKNOWLEDGMENTS

Somehow it's very strange that books always start with the acknowledgments. The start of the book is never really the time you need all the people that are acknowledged. It's when the newness of the project wears off and you realize that there's nothing but hard work ahead that you really appreciate the support that these people provide.

This book is no different. Like any long project, it turns out to be the work of many hands, all of them working in separate and important ways to fashion the finished product.

Without the stories of Wayne Hoppe, Bill Hoppe, and Fred Huber, this book would have lacked life. Without the information offered by people like Warren Johnson and George Athas, it wouldn't have been complete. There were proofreaders like Doug Laubach and Ralph Saunders who offered their critiques and encouragement.

A book without original artwork really isn't worth buying and John Potter outdid himself on this one, providing a beautiful cover and original pen-and-ink drawings throughout.

Good friend and great wildlife cinematographer Gordon Eastman offered his verbal words of encouragement and the written words that make up the introduction to *The Elk Hunter*. And there is Ralph Staton who has done so much to help put cow calls, bull calls, and other products of E.L.K., Inc., in hunters' hands throughout the West.

The photographic talents of Mike Francis, Bob Zellar, and Frank Martin help brighten the pages along with the invaluable collection of old photographs from Doris Whithorn and Dick Herriford.

There are people who helped us learn about elk along the way like Terry and Martha Lonner, Graham Taylor, Fred King, Phil Schladweiler, Charlie Eustace, and Dick Mackie. And there were others like Wayne Schile, Dick Wesnick, and Warren Rogers whose encouragement and support did much to help a writing career.

And, there are the hunting partners who played a role in so many of the experiences you'll read about in the pages to come. These characters are people like Keith Wheat, Rod Churchwell, Mark Wright, Bill Marchington, Vince Yannone, Mike Fillinger, Arnold Lyon, Art Hobart, Curt Collins, Rob Seelye, and John Kremer. With their help, we became elk hunters. Without them, getting there wouldn't have been nearly as much fun.

Finally, there are the home folks. Our wives, Dee Laubach and Carol Henckel, put up with plenty as the manuscript of this book took shape. And our kids, Wade, Kirk, Lori, and Ryan in Gardiner and Andy and Matt in Park City, kept us going, fueled our hunting efforts and brought a breath of fresh air to the endeavor as each reached hunting age.

To all these people, for the roles they played when we needed them most, we humbly give thanks.

■

FOREWORD

"Duck, Don, duck!"

"Jump, Mark, jump! You call that a jump?"

Whew, there's nothing worse than a rifle or bow-toting woman who feels she's been scorned. So before we go any further—and to avoid any elk droppings hurled at us—let's get a few things straight.

We didn't mean to insult Peggy, Donna, Patty, or any other woman who happens to be an elk hunter with the way this book is written. But they'll probably notice that after using the word hunter, we start using pronouns like "his" or "him" on the second reference. That's not meant to be a slight. We just did it so the book would read more smoothly.

In truth, we discussed that issue and even had plans to fully de-sex the writing. We could have used the word "outdoorperson" for one hunter or "outdoorpeoplepersons" for more than one. We talked about using "unisexgunner" or even "hunterhumanoid." But we finally scrapped all those plans. Don figured that he'd get his tongue too badly twisted when he tried to say them into the speaker of his tape recorder. Mark knew he'd never spell them write when it came to righting the book.

So we went with the dread "his" and "him," knowing full well that there might be a few elk droppings thrown our way because of it. That's why we're going through the practice sessions.

Just as we did in our other book, *Elk Talk*, we also opted to use the universal "I" when referring to the experiences of either of us. Once again, it seemed so much cleaner than "Don did this" or "Mark did that." And using the word "Don-Mark" seemed so much like the hunter was some kind of Scandinavian.

For that reason, Don is "I." And Mark is "I." Anyone who's called "my good friend" or "my partner" is just a friend or partner of one of us who the other may not have had the pleasure of meeting yet. As for the term "my son," rest assured there has been no hanky-panky by either of us.

Lucky for you, and for us, Gordon Eastman, who so graciously wrote the introduction for this book, can be himself. As perhaps the most adventurous wildlife cinematographer of our times, his position is secure. He doesn't need to worry about pronouns.

With all those semantics behind, both we and now I hope you enjoy *The Elk Hunter*. The book is designed to follow the development of an elk hunter from his first, faltering steps down the trail. It will share what he learns along the way to help him become a consistently successful elk hunter. There are basic lessons, some new insights, and the latest in elk hunting tactics that are being used by veteran elk hunters. I'll spend a little time talking about some options to make your hunt more exciting. And I'll finish up with a discussion of what happens at the end of the trail.

Along with its companion volume, *Elk Talk*, I feel that *The Elk Hunter* will give you the most complete view of practical knowledge on elk and elk hunting in print today. While the authors both hail from Montana, the book provides information that will work as well in Alberta as it does in Arizona or anywhere else elk can be found on this continent. And it's my fondest hope that when you're done, what you have read here will serve you well in all your elk hunting seasons to come.

> Don Laubach
> Gardiner, Montana
>
> Mark Henckel
> Park City, Montana

INTRODUCTION

By Gordon Eastman

For forty years, I have been an avid outdoor book collector of Western Americana, early exploration, and natural history. I collected all over America as I toured with my wildlife films. Out of all the thousands of books I collected, I consider less than ten percent of them great books. You know what I mean, the type that you read over and over and then pass on to your best friends.

The Elk Hunter is a great book.

What does it take to make a great book? In my opinion, it has to be so readable that time flies to the point that two hours seem like minutes. At the same time, it has to be filled with enough new knowledge and information that I am satisfied with the time spent reading it. But the most important ingredient is that it has to be honest. So many of the outdoor books written today are compiled from library research, not from real life experiences. Research is the easy part. The hard part is living and remembering these real life experiences. *The Elk Hunter* has all of these.

Don Laubach has been my friend for the past twenty years. Whether we have been fishing the Yellowstone River or hunting whitetail bucks in the north, I have always marveled at his ability to analyze, and put into perspective, all the big and little episodes that happen in the outdoor world. Then he was able to file them away for future reference.

Don also is not a one-season person. He participates and enjoys the outdoors all year long. He built a cabin on a mountain at nine thousand feet elevation, just so he could observe not only elk, but all the wildlife that surrounds it throughout the year. He and his wife, Dee, snowshoe into the cabin in the middle of winter just to check up on Mother Nature and make sure she's still taking care of things there. And if you are ever fortunate enough to visit the cabin in the summer, you will see the delight in their eyes as they watch the hummingbirds work the meadows they have planted in wildflowers. Don has lived his life in the center of the greatest elk hunting and habitat in North America and remembers it all.

One of the best things about *The Elk Hunter* is that it seems to fit the hunters that read it no matter what their experience level. There is plenty of information to get the newcomer started. And the veteran will learn some new tactics and let the book help him remember the experiences he had himself in the mountains. When I was reading the chapter entitled "Stalking the Black Timber" it brought back memories of twenty years ago when I lived on a little ranch at the base of the Teton Mountains. It was the second week of elk season and I was out walking with my daughter when we heard two bulls duel with their bugles from the black timber on the mountainside behind our home. I rushed back and put on my moccasins, grabbed my rifle, and spent the next few hours sneaking on these two fine trophies. The book brought back all these great memories for me and I am sure there will be episodes in this book that will jog your memory of the good times you have spent in the outdoors.

If any of you are fortunate enough to read *The Billings Gazette,* you will be familiar with Mark Henckel's by-line. You will have to agree with me that he is one of the most knowledgeable outdoor writers of today. Mark is a great editor, as well, and his books flow with grace and are punctuated with humor. I like to think of him as Montana's Mark Twain of the outdoors.

The combination of Mark's writing ability and Don's outdoor experiences make this book one that you will keep for your grandchildren to enjoy. For me, that is the mark of a great book.

■

THE ELK HUNTER

You can be born rich. You can be born poor. You can be born handsome. Or you can be born ugly. But you can't be born an elk hunter.

Somewhere along the way, you have to make the fateful decision that you want to become an elk hunter. At that point in time, you embark on a trail that has been walked by many in the past. But each hunter walks the trail differently.

Some hunters are lucky enough to grow up in elk country and learn the game from their elders. Others opt for the sport when they're already full grown. Some live in elk country. Some do not. However you start down the trail, you have to suffer through some growing pains.

For my own part, I can remember distinctly the dreams that I had when I first picked up my rifle and my baptism in elk hunting arrived. Instead of being humble, I dreamed about just the elk that I wanted to shoot. I wanted chocolate brown antlers with polished tips. I wanted a good bull. Not a monster, mind you. But I wanted a good, solid five-point bull. Until that elk came along, I was going to let all others go past me. I'd be patient and wait for the one I wanted. If I only knew then what I know now.

Elk hunting has a way of humbling the beginner. Your dreams don't always pan out. The first steps you make on the trail are likely to be shaky ones. You'll make your first mistakes, like dreaming about just the elk that you want. You'll find that elk country is a big, big place and that elk are not to be found everywhere within it. And by the time your first experiences are tucked away in your mind, the elk and the country they live in will teach you the lesson of humility that for most hunters, elk never come easy.

But this realization is something that should be taken in stride. After all, you have to start somewhere and there's no place better to do your starting than at the beginning.

If you really want to be an elk hunter, you'll sit back and reevaluate the situation. You'll set some goals for yourself. You'll start gleaning information wherever you can. You'll add to your storehouse of knowledge in countless ways. And, in the process, you'll have taken your first fateful steps down the trail to becoming the elk hunter of your dreams.

So You Want to Be an Elk Hunter

In the dim, faraway past, I can remember a simpler time. There was no elk hunting then. Instead, ruffed grouse exploded from grape thickets with thundering wings. Rushing streams splashed with the sounds of rising trout. And white-tailed deer gave a tentative twitch of the tail, then bounded off into the gathering dusk.

These were pleasant years of the autumnal innocence of my youth, when rod and gun blended with colored leaves, crisp mornings and warm afternoons to produce a varied mosaic of fall days in the field.

Then, the curse arrived.

Yes, I'll confess it. Elk hunting is a curse. It's a delightful curse, maybe, but a curse nevertheless. It's the type of curse, in fact, that can grow to fill your every waking minute and every sleeping hour, your day in the workplace, your night at home, your weekend getaway, your family vacation, your mother-in-law's birthday, your wife's anniversary, and everything else that matters little compared to the almighty elk. You see elk, hear elk, smell elk, think elk, and think you see, hear, and smell elk. It's a powerful, powerful curse. But, believe me, if you've got to be cursed, this is the only way to go.

If you don't believe elk hunting is a curse, you've never seen the wild-eyed characters that inhabit elk country in autumn. Their faces and clothes will be soiled beyond recognition. They won't have seen a razor or a shower in days. And they'll mumble about big bulls over in the next drainage, herd after herd of cows without an antler in sight, and an endless search for the elk of their dreams. Yet these are only the mild crazies. They're out during the elk season, when they're supposed to be.

The hard-core crazies are out there stalking the slopes in all seasons, spending days, weeks, and months in the company of elk just to pick up a few more pieces of the puzzle that elk hunting presents to elk hunters. You talk about wild. If you find the wild-eyed elk hunter of November a bit strange, just imagine the chigger-bitten, foot-sore, sweat-stained, dirt-smeared, tick-infested elk hunter of June. It is a chilling thought.

And you say you want to be an elk hunter yourself? A dedicated, dyed-in-the-wool, consistently successful elk hunter? Think hard before you reply. We're talking about shaping your future here. We're talking about innocence lost, lost forever. In fact, we're talking about a whole new way of life that can carry you from your youth to your retirement, sometimes all in the same season with an elk tag still in your pocket.

If it sounds like I'm being a little melodramatic here, rest assured it isn't because I don't want any more competition in elk country once the season begins. I'm not trying to scare you off. It's just that if you want the curse, you'd better realize the curse you're getting yourself into. Elk hunting can be extremely contagious. It can spread like a festering disease through every facet of your life. And, frankly, it takes a lot of time and patience and work if you're going to be consistently successful at the game.

So, if you want to be an elk hunter, I figured you might as well get the bad news first. And if the bad news sounds very, very bad, well, the good news sounds very, very good, too. The rewards of elk hunting are many indeed.

The sights and smells of a high country dawn aren't soon forgotten. Neither is the feel of saddle leather after several hours on a mountain trail. The crackle and glow of a warm campfire surrounded by friends is a scene that can't easily be erased from memory. And, of course, there are the elk themselves. The calf which calls for its mother further up the slope. The lead cow, with its years of savvy, leading her herd to safety. And, the mature bull of every hunter's dreams, outlined against the evening sky of the Rocky Mountain West. Heady, heady stuff. Bright, crisp images painted on the canvas of the outdoors at its best.

It's really no wonder that elk hunting has become the prime obsession of so many in recent years. It is one of the last great challenges facing a hunter. It's also one of the few which seems to get better with time. The more miles of trail that are put behind you, the more you grow to appreciate the elk themselves and the hunts that go with them. It's definitely a sport you can grow with and one that will grow within you as you stalk the wilderness trails year after year and watch the passage of time in the high country through your binoculars or spotting scope.

Elk hunters enter this world in several different ways. It might be at the start of their life, tagging along as a youngster when their fathers or uncles head into the field. Others may turn it into a young person's sport of choice, a lifelong avocation sparked by a career move into an elk state. Still others may look at elk hunting as a once-in-a-lifetime experience to be enjoyed after they've matured as a veteran hunter of other species. The entry time can make a big difference, but one thing remains the same. Elk country is a big and mysterious place the first time you see it with rifle in hand.

Simply put, elk aren't easy. The country they live in isn't easy. And the hunter who can put the elk puzzle together immediately with a bull to hang his tag on has been both blessed with great luck and lulled into a false sense of security that he really understands the situation. Continue in the game a little longer and you'll find the humbling truth that you still have much to learn if initial success is to become a habit.

Perhaps the easiest way to become a consistently successful elk hunter is to grow up with it. The youngster who grows up in elk country has been more than twice blessed. Time, for example, is on his side right from the start. Years and years lie ahead of him to learn his lessons well. His resources include relatives who may hunt elk, hunting areas to explore nearby, and the old-timers who are usually on the lookout for young ears to hear time-worn tales of past glory.

Perhaps the best way to become an elk hunter is to grow up in elk country and learn as you grow up. Scott Hamilton photo.

It's in these tales of current seasons and seasons past that a young hunter or hunter-to-be picks up his first pieces of the elk hunting puzzle. Bits of wisdom are gathered here and gleaned there and filed away in the unconscious of the young to be drawn upon when situations present themselves in the years to come. As the elk challenge grows within them, they can strike out and learn the territory. In their teen years, they can explore on their own and surpass even the knowledge of their elders, if they want to. And by the time they reach their adulthood, they can already have become veterans of the mountains, ready to tackle even the cagiest of bulls in their quest for elk.

If there's a drawback in all this, it's that we have no choice in our birth. The when and where and to whom are left up to Someone Else. And we just as easily could be born in Big City, East State, to Clem and Clementine Nonhunter, as to hunting parents in elk country.

Some dreamers solve the problem of their birth by simply

Elk country is a big and mysterious place for the hunter who sees it for the first time. Frank R. Martin photo.

moving to elk country once they reach their adulthood. They're already behind in the game to the lucky-by-birth, and they know it. But at least they've arrived, ready, willing, and able to let the elk hunting curse have at them. What this group may lack in breeding and chance, they more than make up for in enthusiasm.

This newcomer to elk country at least has the resources of the elk world to call upon to guide him. He or she can read all the books. They can buy and study the maps. They can walk the trails in and out of season searching for elk. They can usually get first crack at the elk licenses over the nonresidents. They have the locals to pump for information and the veteran hunters to answer their questions. And, best of all, they know that in time, they will become a local themselves. When that happens, they will be privvy to the things that only locals know and talk about among themselves.

Being a newcomer to elk country isn't the worst of situations at all. It just means that you have the opportunity to invest the time and effort to become a consistently successful elk hunter. All you need is the wild look in your eyes the minute somebody starts talking about elk and the driving desire to make elk hunting your way of life.

A far tougher road lies ahead for the visitor to elk country. For the nonresident hunter, it may be a once-in-a-lifetime hunt or an every-year-in-a-lifetime habit. In either event, there are hurdles along the way that must be cleared to find happiness and success in elk hunting.

Too often, the nonresident comes in with too little knowledge of the animal he's hunting and the area he has chosen for that hunt. Too often, they have shortchanged themselves in time, allotting too few days in the field. Their expectations of the hunt and the elk themselves are often virtually unattainable. Their search for elk hunting happiness will surely end in gloom.

It's no slap at the visitor to elk country to report these things. It's the stark reality that most of them come frightfully unprepared for the experiences that will face them. They often haven't ever done it before. They haven't read everything they could about it. They haven't talked in depth with an outfitter, if they do indeed hire one, or another knowledgeable source to get a true picture of what lies ahead in terms of available elk, camp life, physical demands, proper equipment, and the myriad small details on which happiness and success are built.

Sometimes, the best of times lies further down the trail on the visitor's second, third, fourth, or fifth journey to elk country. Too often, however, a sour first experience may mean the return trips never come to pass. Enough knowledge beforehand can spell the difference in whether or not the full effect of the curse is allowed to take hold on the visitor to elk country.

Remember, what we're talking about here is the curse of elk hunting, something that's so pleasantly pervasive that you can't help but get caught up by it once you take your first few serious steps into the elk world. As I've said before, there are many ways to catch the curse by hunters of all ages and backgrounds. The important thing is to make it a decision of choice. If you're going to start, make sure it is something you want to grow in and have become a part of your life. And, finally, make sure you take your steps in the right direction so the trail will lead you toward your goals.

When you pick up your rifle and head into elk country, you're leaving behind the comfortable, autumnal innocence of other hunters and fishermen. It's a whole new world of difficult challenges, physical demands, rigorous study, and, of course, the sensual delights that can only be found in the high country that elk call home.

Elk country is no place for the faint of heart. And becoming a consistently successful elk hunter is no task for anybody short of a wild-eyed crazy. It's a life-changing curse I wouldn't want to wish on anybody—except you and me.

These Trails Were Walked Before

Most hunters enjoy fantasies about the good old days. They sit on a mountaintop, look off into the faraway haze, and dream about what it must have been like a century ago in their chosen hunting country. Elk hunters are no different, especially novice elk hunters. Once they see the breadth and scope of elk country and get their first taste of hunting for elk, they get caught up in the romance of the whole thing. Their minds wander to make-believe times in what they feel must be elk hunting's colorful past. They figure elk must have been everywhere. And, in some ways, those hunters are right.

If you go far enough back in time, there were six subspecies of elk in North America, the Rocky Mountain, Roosevelt, Manitoban, Eastern, Tule, and Merriam. They roamed, in varying concentrations, all across most parts of what would become the United States and Canada. But talk about those subspecies, you have to go way back to the time before white men learned that elk meat was fine table fare. Once 17th, 18th, and 19th century settlers found that elk were good to eat, that their hides could be bought and sold, and that their stained ivory teeth made fancy decorations, the elk's fate was sealed. They went the way of the passenger pigeon in all but a few select areas of the Rockies and the Pacific Northwest.

In fact, widespread availability of good populations of elk in recent times is pretty much a product of the 20th century. Elk transplants, most of them from the Gardiner, Montana, and Jackson, Wyoming, areas and nearby Yellowstone and Grand Teton national parks, were responsible for bringing elk back to

Elk were loaded on trains at Gardiner, Montana, and shipped throughout the West to repopulate areas where elk had disappeared. Doris Whithorn photo.

the mountains of the West and other parts of the country. Because of the decimation of other elk subspecies, just about the only huntable elk we talk about today are the Rocky Mountain and Roosevelt elk, with the Roosevelt living in the mountains of the Pacific Northwest and the Rocky Mountain spread throughout the Rockies of the United States and Canada. Other huntable populations are limited indeed and strictly the result of transplants from the Rockies.

Because so few elk made it past the years of settlement, most elk hunting is living its good old days right now. The end result of the transplants and the benefits of wildlife management have provided more opportunities for more elk in more places than at any time in the past hundred years. Aside from scattered herds which survived the onslaught of farmers', ranchers', and miners' guns, and the land-altering changes of development, most elk populations are relatively new in time. Many, in fact, may be only decades old. And the hunters who are dreaming of times past may find that there wasn't much of a past to dream about where they hunt.

That doesn't mean there isn't a colorful history to elk hunting itself, however. If you just pick the right place to do your dreaming, you can find more local color than you ever imagined. Gardiner, Montana, is certainly one of those places where you can gain a little historical perspective on where we've been in the past.

The Gardiner area, on the northern edge of Yellowstone National Park, has always been elk hunting country, thanks for the most part to the park itself which was set aside by Congress in 1872. Here, elk never disappeared, and though their numbers fluctuated over time, there was always a big enough population to support widespread hunting.

It was to Gardiner, for example, that then-President Teddy Roosevelt came in 1903 to dedicate the arch at the park's north gate and do a little elk hunting while he happened to be in the neighborhood. It was here, too, where the rich hunters from the East came to put those big trophy heads on the wall. And it was here where my dad headed when it came time in 1915 to put away a supply of meat for the winter.

Grandfather was a homesteader, trying to scratch out a living in the Crazy Mountains nearly one hundred miles to the north and east of Gardiner. There were no elk in the Crazies then and few deer as well. So he sent his three sons in a horse-drawn wagon for the three-day ride to hunting country. They hunted in the Slip 'n Slide Drainage. And, according to my dad's recollection, they bagged three elk after several days' hunting. They then loaded their elk and rode the three days back to the Crazy Mountains, after stopping to buy hay in Emigrant along the way. As I recall, the story went that my dad always felt he got took on that hay purchase. But then I guess he probably wasn't the first hunter to feel he was taken while away from home on a hunting trip. And, whether we like it or not, I'm sure he won't be the last.

No one ever told me, but I'm sure the three elk that were carried in the back of that wagon were all cows. It wasn't that my dad wasn't good enough to bag a bull. It's just that in those days, almost everyone bagged cows by choice. Bulls were lean and tough. Cows were fat and tender. And considering the fact they were shooting elk for meat, it's unlikely they would have taken a winter's worth of lean and tough eating by choice. That tendency to shoot cows

In the early days of this century, hunters traveled to and from elk country by train. Doris Whithorn photo.

instead of bulls was the hard and fast rule, rather than the exception, in those days.

If there was a difference in his hunt, it was the fact that he came here by wagon. In the early days of this century, most hunters came to elk country by train. There was a railroad spur that split off the old Northern Pacific line at Livingston and headed southward to Gardiner and Yellowstone Park. Hunters would catch a ride on the train and be dropped off at various points along the way to do their hunting. Then, when they got their elk, they would load it back on the train for the trip back to other parts of Montana or points further east. It was a colorful scene, with the hunters and their elk, and a romantic time to be an elk hunter. But most elk taken were still cows, shot by the local miners or others from inside and outside the area. The miners would shoot them all year and elk remains can still be found beside their rotting old cabins. The hunters would come out in fall and early winter and do the same.

If there's a surprising aspect of elk hunting, it's how long the desire to shoot only cows hung on. Wayne Hoppe, for example, was born in the Gardiner area and helped his grandfather, Walter, and father, Paul, in the guiding business before taking it up himself after World War II. He was in on more elk kills than even he can remember and yet he said this tendency toward cows lingered on all through his outfitting career which ran until 1965. Hunters he took out would literally ride their horses past herds of a hundred bulls without shooting. They wouldn't shoot them because they didn't want to eat them.

If a bull was shot, one of the key parts of field dressing was to chop off the antlers so they didn't hang up in the brush when the bull was dragged out. Those antlers were all left behind. After all, you already had the weight of the meat to pack out. Why bother adding the weight of the antlers?

In his own mind, Hoppe is sure that countless record book elk were taken in that country without anyone ever knowing it. He can remember seeing many bulls with eight and nine points to a side that never had a rifle pointed in their direction. He can also remember a bull which was shot that had a spread of sixty-four-and-a-quarter inches which allowed four men to stand between the antlers to have their picture taken. The size of the antlers on those bulls was simply because of their long lives. With no one shooting at them, their antlers grew to maximum maturity. One bull that was taken by a hunter near Gardiner in the late 1940s had been tagged at Jackson, Wyoming, some twenty-eight years earlier.

Most hunters who sought these elk were simply laying in a supply of meat for the winter. For some rich eastern hunters, however, the sport did involve bringing back a big set of antlers to hang over the fireplace. But they were the minority. And even some of these were more interested in the meat. All the locals and most of the regulars from outside the area were meat hunters, pure and simple. Their joy was in the pounds of venison they brought back home. The amount of sport involved in doing that was left up to the individual.

To truly appreciate the scene that was going on every fall in elk country, you have to take a peek back in time to the way the tiny town of Gardiner was in those years. And believe me, in those years, Gardiner was wild. In elk season, the bars never closed. Gambling casinos were wide-open. The hotels were full. Hunters slept in every available corner of any room in any establishment that would tolerate them. A good deal of the restaurant fare was elk meat mixed with beef tallow. Frankly, many hunters never

Hunters chained up their two-wheel drive vehicles and headed toward the firing line in search of cows. Roy Walton photo

made it out of town to where the elk were being hunted. They went home with elk that were shot by someone else.

In this day and age of more straight-laced accordance to hunting rules and ethics, the notion of drunken hunters, burping up elk burgers, and sleeping in the corner of a bar after they lost all their money gambling, should seem pretty wild. But, in truth, it wasn't any wilder than the things going on out on the hunt.

The bulk of the elk hunting then was done during the winter migration when deep snows forced the elk out of Yellowstone Park and headed them toward their wintering grounds further north. When word spread that the migration was on, hunters would flock to the area by the hundreds, creating a firing line situation which was almost as dangerous for the hunters as it was for the elk. During the late 1930s, '40s, and '50s, hunters would drive out from town, forming long lines of cars waiting for the 8 a.m. start when the gates would be opened to the hunting area. These lines of cars, most of them with their wheels chained, would snake up the trails toward the waiting elk. If one car got stuck, other hunters would lift it off the trail and set it in the deep snow so the rest of the cars could continue.

Once the elk were located, they would often be surrounded and the shooting would begin. With hunters on all sides, the elk would run one way, then another, and finally mill around out in the middle of the open valleys. Amid the hail of bullets flying in every direction, it's amazing that hunters weren't killed along with the elk. But, surprisingly, the casualties of those firing line years were rare though more than a few survivors still tell tales of hiding behind rocks or pressing their bodies into the snow when the bullets started whizzing past.

To give a little more depth to the scene, you should understand that not everyone on the firing line was a hunter. Some of them didn't even have guns. The old saying was that if you just showed up with your tag and a good pair of running shoes, you could get yourself a pretty good elk. In fact, a joke at the time was told about a fashion-conscious woman wearing a fur coat who stumbled and fell while running toward an elk and was tagged twice herself before she could get back on her feet.

The firing line led to some frightening slaughters. Wayne Hoppe can recall days when his hunters took twenty, thirty, and forty elk. He remembers the day on Eagle Creek in the winter of 1946-47 when there was a count of 1,280 elk killed before noon. It was a time in elk hunting history when a man with a gun and elk out in front of him would keep firing until he either ran out of cartridges or all the elk were on the ground. To do less would be considered selfish. It was also a time when nobody gave it a second thought if you took home an elk even if the extent of your hunting gear was just a tag and a knife. Hunters with friends, in fact, would annually tag an elk even when they never made it out of the bars or gambling casinos.

If all that sounds like bad sportsmanship on display, you have to remember that sport wasn't necessarily the all-important driving factor for these people. Elk were an animal to be harvested for their meat just like beef cattle, hogs, or sheep. It didn't matter so much how you gathered that meat, as long as you had the meat to take home when the hunt was over. The hunting trips themselves were supposed to be fun, so why not have your fun in town, and, if you could, leave the meat-gathering to your friends.

All the colorful past of elk country was just that, a colorful past, whether you're talking about the hunting at Gardiner, Montana, or Jackson, Wyoming, or the scattered other places where you could hunt elk a half-century and longer ago. It was as romantic as traveling by train from Back East and as frightening as the firing line.

But it didn't really have much to do with the fantasies of heading out in the old days with rifle in hand in search of big bulls. The assault on the big bulls came later. The drive to put your name in the record books with the really big bulls came even later than that.

In the old days, meat hunting was a way of life whether you were hunting elk in the Appalachians, central Canada, the upper Midwest, or the Rockies. It led to the demise of some elk populations and, in terms of today, was an unsporting approach to the resource that remained in other parts of elk country.

It's true that these elk hunting trails were walked before. But it's a different kind of hunter who sets out on these trails today. And the type of hunter you are, want to become, or hope someday to be, is another consideration to be studied closely and carefully before you pick up your rifle and head out for elk.

Meat or Trophy Hunter

Close your eyes for a moment and picture the elk of your dreams. Is it a big bull, a six-point or seven-point monster? Is it a dry cow, any old cow, or maybe a plump spike? Most hunters these days would go with the big bull. Those wide, sweeping antlers have a way of casting a spell over a hunter more than any other facet of the sport. But before we're done with this little exercise, close your eyes again. Now, picture the elk you'd be willing to pull the trigger on, when you have it in your sights. Think about it. And be honest with yourself. Have the size of the antlers withered a bit? Have they disappeared entirely?

It's no disgrace to admit you'd settle for something less than a record book bull. It doesn't make you a better person to decide to take a record book bull or nothing. The important thing is to come up with some sort of goal before you head into the mountains looking for elk. It will make things easier for you, easier for your partners, and easier for your guide, if you decide to hire one. But the decision itself might not be an easy one to make.

The reason for the difficulty is that elk hunting has changed a great deal in recent years and continues to change. It's no wonder some hunters are unsure of what they're looking for. In the old

A hunter has to set goals for himself, whether it's a cow, spike, or trophy bull, before starting his hunt. Bob Zellar photo.

days, it was almost always a matter of putting away a supply of meat for the winter. For the best eating, that always turned out to be fat cows. In fact, a dry cow, one which didn't have a calf that year, was considered the best possible target.

Even as recently as twenty years ago, the rule of thumb in most hunting camps was that whoever got shooting should continue to shoot until all the elk were on the ground. To pass up shots at any legal elk when others had tags to fill was considered to be selfish and a hunter just might not be invited back to elk camp the following year if he persisted in such behavior.

Certainly, even in the old days, there were exceptions to the rule. Some hunters wouldn't think of having someone else fill their tags. Some hunters, especially those from Back East, also would pass up the cows and spikes in search of a big bull. But these trophy hunters were looked upon as being a bit eccentric and certainly not part of the mainstream of elk hunting life. For most of elk hunting's history, the old saying, "You can't eat the antlers," was very liberally applied to anyone who called himself a trophy hunter.

This recent past has left today's elk hunter in a state of transition. There are still hunters who want cows. There are some that will take any legal elk. But, more and more, being a trophy hunter seems to be the latest rage. Everyone seems to be looking for the monster bulls and game managers are being constantly pressed to increase the number of these trophy elk in the population. In fact, the measure of a hunter seems to be determined in increments of six points to a side. If you shoot a six-point bull, you've made it in the hunting world. Shoot anything less and you simply haven't arrived as a full-fledged elk hunter yet.

The benefit and curse of this kind of trophy hunting is that a hunter forces himself to be selective. He's not going to blow away any elk that happens to wander within view. He'll pass on the raghorns and five-points. He may not even shoot a small six-point, waiting instead for the big herd bulls to show themselves. That hunter may not always come out of the mountains with an elk to show for his efforts, but when he does, it's always a dandy that anyone would be proud to hang on their wall.

But for most hunters who start out in the game, the question of being a meat hunter, trophy hunter, or something in between isn't easy to answer. Yet it's vital that a hunter decides the issue

The Elk Hunter ■

If you want only trophy bulls, you have to realize that you'll be battling tall odds in filling your elk tag. Michael H. Francis photo.

before he takes his rifle in hand.

Some beginners, for example, set their sights on a six-point bull not knowing how difficult it is to come up with one of these bulls. They head into the mountains with bright promise that if they just put in a little extra effort, that six-point will be theirs. Then, after a few days, weeks, or months, they come home disappointed because they've worked so hard and have nothing to show for their efforts. It's discouraging enough to some that they may never return to elk country.

Other hunters adjust their goals along the way. Six-points, become five-points, become spikes, become anything legal as their hunting time gets shorter. But these hunters may waste a lot of time and several opportunities before they reach their final goal.

But as any veteran elk hunter can tell you, opportunitites at elk should never be wasted. They may not return for a long, long time. And elk hunting luck is a fickle entity indeed.

One friend, for example, had been taking his week of vacation in elk season for twenty years, hunting an area where branch-antlered bulls were the only legal game. In those twenty years, he has never filled his elk tag. He bumped into plenty of cows. He shot deer along the way. But the bull of his dreams never did materialize. Call it bad luck. Call it whatever you want. But don't forget to call it a most frustrating facet of anyone's hunting career.

The need to set goals for yourself is also critical in other ways. If you're a trophy hunter, you have to be assured that the area you pick has trophy bulls in it to start with. Nonresidents, especially, can be caught in that trap. They line up an outfitter over long distance telephone lines in hopes of bagging a Boone and Crockett bull, only to end up in a hunting camp with a great history of taking spikes and raghorns and little else. What a horrible waste of time, money, and high blood pressure medication. If you're simply hunting for meat, elk density becomes a more important issue than antler size. You could care less how many record book bulls come out of an area. Instead, you want to know how many elk are there and what hunter success percentages can be expected. You want to know whether shooting cows is permitted. You want to know if you can shoot spikes. You want to broaden the possibilities instead of restricting them to particular Boone and Crockett scores.

Another consideration for the hunter is exactly what you plan to do with the elk you shoot. In the old days, that was never a problem. You were going to take the elk home, cut it into steaks, roasts, and chops, and have the rest ground into hamburger. Then you were going to eat it. These days, for some hunters, it seems the eating is almost secondary to the trophy itself. Many, in fact, have no idea what they're going to do with the meat. Often, they just give it away to whoever will take it off their hands. Or they pay to have it made into jerky, salami, or some type of game sausage. The salami and sausage route has saved many a trophy hunter from having to face tough old bull on the end of his fork. But, with a good sausage maker to help him, I guess you could also say that hunter had his antlers and still came up with good eating.

In the end, the decision on what your goals should be must be made by each individual hunter. It's a product of soul-searching and deciding what you really want out of your elk hunting experience. For some hunters, that decision may be theirs alone. For others, it could be affected by outside factors in their lives.

If elk hunting is an every-year thing, there's no reason to believe that your goals must stay the same. Many hunters, for example, find happiness by revising their goals along the way. Some try to improve on the last elk they took. The logical progression from spike to raghorn to five-point to six-point can't always be guaranteed, however. If your first elk is a record book bull, you may wait a long time before ever pulling the trigger again at something bigger. You may also weaken after a number of spikes present themselves as easy targets and finally decide that a spike in hand is worth six-points that stay far in the bush.

Having a family to feed on a daily basis is another very real consideration for the elk hunter. It's hard to argue with several hundred pounds of cow when you look around the dinner table and see all those hungry faces looking back at you. For many of us who live and raise our children in elk country, family responsibilities both create our hunting preferences and open possibilities as well. That's certainly one of the reasons why I was brought up as a meat hunter and still have strong tendencies in that direction. It's not that I won't take aim at a six-point bull when it presents itself. But I won't necessarily pass up the spikes, raghorns, or even a fat cow if given the chance with a tag in my pocket.

Back when I started hunting, bringing home the winter supply of meat was important. In those days, the rule was still to shoot elk when you saw them to fill your partners' tags. Meat hunting was the rule. Elk meat is still important when my family sits down to dinner. And it's hard to argue with a platter of juicy steaks when someone tries to tell me that it's too bad I didn't get a big bull instead of that four or five-point.

For the young hunter, I wouldn't offer anything but praise for any kind of legal elk that's brought home. In my own mind, I honestly feel that their bringing home an elk can actually bring a family together. It allows the younger members to be providers, too, and when dinner time arrives, they can take pride in the fact that it's their hunting success which has helped feed the family. In short, it becomes a family affair to put away the winter's supply

Even a spike bull is a highly regarded trophy for some hunters who set their sights on one. Michael H. Francis photo.

of meat.

There's another positive aspect to the family approach to elk hunting which is an additional blessing of living in elk country. As the kids get older and begin finding their own success in elk hunting, the old man can hunt trophies if he chooses. By then, there may be fewer mouths to feed around the table and more hunters ready to help fill the larder. It's time to kick back and do what you please.

At that time, the hunter's goals may have changed. But, there still will be goals. Trophy hunter, meat hunter, or anything in between, goals are something you can't do without in elk hunting, whether you're a novice headed out for your first hunt or a veteran of many decades in the mountains. You have to know what you want before you pull the trigger. To do that, you should be satisfied within yourself at the goals you've set, before you ever pick up a gun.

■

THIS IS ELK HUNTING

If you're going to be an elk hunter, you've got to look like one. You've got to talk like one. You've got to have some sense of what's going on.

But usually, as soon as someone finds out that you're a novice elk hunter, you're going to get more information on the subject than you ever wanted. Some of that information will be good. Some will be badly outdated.

All you can do is struggle along and try to pick out the trees from the forest. It's a good thing to learn some things about the past. Elk hunting was much different then. Yet many of the old tactics and even some of the old equipment can still be used today.

But if you want to make things easier on yourself, at least be aware that there are some new things on the market too. Most successful elk hunters will make use of modern technology whenever it suits their needs. If they didn't make the change, there would still be hunters out there with spears and clubs trying to outdo the hunters with high-powered rifles.

Today's rifle calibers allow a hunter to shoot a powerful bullet in a flat trajectory for a long, long way. They're devastatingly accurate and you can take aim at an elk in any reasonable range with extreme confidence.

Today's light fibers and fabrics and clothing construction also make life in elk country far more comfortable than it was in the old days. You can stay warm and dry. You can walk quietly. You can tailor your clothing and equipment to the hunting you plan to do.

Often, a novice hunter will make his first contact with elk at this stage of development. Often, he will make his first miss, too. But as a novice hunter, you have to realize that you're still in the formative stage. You're gathering the knowledge that will help you further down the road.

If you have patience, you'll wait for that knowledge to bear fruit on its own. If you don't, you'll hire an outfitter and build your successes on his knowledge. Either way, a novice hunter still doesn't have it all figured out yet. But he's learning, and he's learning fast.

You Seen Any of Them Elks?

The grim reality of the novice elk hunter came to me in the form of a smiling face and a fresh-from-the-box hunter orange jacket on a trail not far from the end of the road. I was walking back to the cluster of cars and trucks parked there at mid-afternoon after long hours of elk hunting. The smiling face was just hitting the trail in all his orange-clad glory, complete with a new rifle slung over his shoulder and squeaky new boots on his feet.

The man stopped on the trail, wanting to talk, so I obliged him. But then the fateful words came from his mouth, the ones I'll never forget. With the openness and honesty of someone who really wanted to know, he asked, "You seen any of them elks? I heard these mountains were just loaded with elks. So I figured I might as well just go get me one."

In a way, the man with the smiling face was almost refreshing in his innocence. After all the days, weeks, months, and years I've spent chasing elk, to have someone put the task in such simple terms was truly amazing. It's almost frightening to think about how many times my search was in vain. It's equally horrifying to think about how much that man with the smiling face had to learn about the sport before he could reasonably expect to find some success at it. But if he was going to innocently ask, I would innocently answer. So I told him that I'd also heard there were some elks in these mountains, but had been out since before dawn without seeing a single bull, cow, or calf. But if I had seen one, I sure would have gotten one of them elks for me, too.

The plight of the novice elk hunter is just that way. They figure if they just go out and hike in elk country, they're going to fill their tag. The veteran elk hunter knows better. If only elk hunting was that easy, we'd all have a big bull hanging from the meat-pole at the end of the trail.

The truth of the matter is that a beginning elk hunter usually has to pay some dues before he finds success. Those dues come in the form of time in the mountains in the company of elk. In fact, of all the factors involved in elk hunting at any level of expertise, time is the single most important one at work. With it comes knowledge, experience, and luck. Without it, the elk hunter is relying totally on luck and that's a fickle commodity indeed that rarely seems to be handy when you need it most.

The thing a beginning elk hunter has to realize is that some of his learning is going to come from the school of hard knocks. It's sad to say, but all the books, videos, cassette tapes, and talk about elk with other hunters simply isn't going to prepare you with everything you need to know. It will give you a big jump on those who haven't made the most of these resources. But you'll still need a large dose of experience to put the pieces of the elk hunting puzzle together.

One of the reasons for the need for first-hand experience to go along with the second-hand experience is that there's nothing that compares to coming face-to-face with an elk. No matter how much you know, it seems to rob the senses of all logic and make us do things we could kick ourselves for later. Some call it elk fever. Others have names for it that are hardly printable. But its effects can be devastating no matter what you call it or when it hits.

One time, for example, I can remember taking a college friend out on his first elk hunt when elk fever took solid hold of the man and robbed the beginning hunter of both his senses and a fine bull. We began our hunt an hour before first light, walking in darkness through the snow-covered mountains to our hunting area. Once there, we cut a single set of tracks and decided to follow them.

The elk that made those tracks was doing everything that elk are supposed to do. He cut through the timbered slopes in pretty much a straight shot, then started to zig-zag when he got close to a stand of some small jackpines. This switchback behavior is a good sign that an elk is nearing his bedding area. And the stands of small jackpines are always prime bedding spots. They're tight enough that an elk is tough to spot in them and because of that, the elk almost always has the upper hand, able to jump and run before a hunter can get his sights on them. So I counseled my friend before we stepped in, telling him that he may only have a moment to get off a shot. In this case, however, both the choice of bedding area and my wise counsel backfired. Instead of stopping there, the elk went through that bunch of jackpines and headed for another a little further down the trail.

We knew the elk pushed on through because we spotted him in one of those rare, beautiful moments. It was a bull, a big six-point, and we caught him between patches of jackpine. He was just standing there, less than fifty yards away, with his head square behind a tree. We could see him. He couldn't see us. We had all of his body before us with a clear shot at the vitals while only his big antlers stuck out from both sides of the tree. It was a shot of which most hunters can only dream. So I whispered to my college friend to take a rest against a tree and shoot.

Elk fever must have taken a terrible grip on my friend. He brought his gun up all right. He took aim. And, he squeezed off a shot. But for some unknown reason, with all that elk to shoot at, he took aim at the bull's head. That head, of course, was still behind the tree. And he smacked that tree square in the trunk, stopping the bullet, spooking the elk, and ruining a beautiful chance at a marvelous bull.

It was a simple case of panic at being so close to such a big animal. It was a horrible miss, the effects of which weren't lost on my friend. He got physically sick to his stomach. He got horribly depressed. His hunting was done for the day and for how much longer after that, I don't really know. A more experienced elk hunter probably would have cursed himself, shaken it off, realized that missing was just part of the game, and continued the hunt for another bull. Instead, I'm sure that miss stayed in his mind for the rest of his life. I know I haven't forgotten it, and I didn't even do the shooting.

I also know, however, that it's upon this type of painful

If elk were easy to locate, it would be easy for every hunter to fill his tag every season.
Michael H. Francis photo

experience which elk hunting knowledge is built. The lesson here was that elk are big animals, that you may be frighteningly close to them, and, yes, that even when you are this close, you still can miss.

In this case, it was a college-age hunter who likely had some hunting experience behind him. There was another time when some of my high school friends had a similar close encounter with elk, only they didn't even have the consolation of a good, solid miss to take home with them.

This time, we also had walked into the hunting area in the dark and were set up near a clearing when the glow of first light revealed there were elk out there feeding. Those elk began to move out as the glow became brighter, signalling both the start of the day and legal shooting time. There was just enough time for a shot before the elk reached the timber, so I touched off a round and downed a big cow. But before dressing it out, I figured if I could only circle around the elk, I might be able to push them back through the timber and to my waiting friends.

The plan worked well. I managed to head them off. And the elk turned back, right toward the spot where my friends were waiting. The only problem was that I didn't hear any shooting.

As it turned out, the elk had come frighteningly close to one friend who was packing an old .30-30 lever action. As the elk came through, he worked that lever action feverishly. But he never pulled the trigger. Tracks revealed that some elk had come within five feet of him. But elk fever engulfed him as those big animals crashed past him and all he had to show for his efforts was a scattering of live rounds on the ground where empty cartridges should have laid. It was another tough lesson for a youngster who could have filled his tag easily.

These lessons aren't limited to the young. Elk fever can strike hunters of any age and, believe me, it can even hit the experienced among us. I can remember taking out an older hunter during one of the late hunts near Gardiner, spotting some elk up ahead, and then sending him over the hill alone to take what I felt might have been the last animal of his career. Hiding behind that hill, I waited for the shot and heard instead what I thought was "Help! Help! Help!" coming from the direction where the man had just gone. It worried me. All I could think of was that the man had become so excited over getting on those elk that he was having a heart attack over there. But when I ran over the hill to help him, I found what he was really saying was "Elk! Elk! Elk!" as he pointed in the direction of the herd without taking a shot.

These experiences, while they may seem funny now, aren't being told to poke fun at those involved. They aren't being told to make me out as an experienced hand who is immune to elk fever, either. In my early hunting days, I can remember mistaking an elk for a horse and not shooting because of it. I can remember when I fancied myself as an expert caller before I really knew what was going on and only managed to kick a herd of elk into high gear by giving them the wrong kind of call. And if I'd have shot every bull that I spooked clear out of the country over the years, people from the Guinness Book of World Records would have beaten a path to my door long ago.

A beginner has to realize that it's going to take some time to sort out the facts about elk. As I said before, elk hunting is like a big puzzle. You pick up pieces here and there, then try to fit them in place. The more pieces you find and put together, the better your chances for success.

Some of those pieces should be surprisingly simple, yet they're not as easy as you might think. You have to train your eyes to see elk, for example. As big as they are, and with the bulls sporting those impressive antlers, you wouldn't think that seeing elk was a problem. But it certainly can be.

There was a time when my daughter drew a special elk permit while she was in high school. Living where we do in the middle of prime elk country, she had been around elk all her life. So it really shouldn't have been a problem when I got her on a herd of elk that had one big bull in its midst.

The herd was only about two hundred yards away. And that bull was heading for the only tree to be seen on the slope across from us where the herd was located. I told her where the bull was and gave her a running description as the bull walked toward the tree, behind the tree, past the tree, and over the hill out of sight. She could see the tree. She just couldn't pick out the bull and ended up not taking a shot.

For me to shoot that elk would have been easy. My daughter even asked me to shoot it for her. But if I had, she would have been robbed of both the opportunity to succeed and the chance to fail. The learning experience would have been lost forever. And it also wouldn't have accomplished the goal we set out for ourselves, that being for her to shoot her first elk.

While not being able to spot that bull out in the open may seem like an extreme case, not being able to spot elk in the timber is far more normal for the beginning elk hunter. In the timber, where elk spend most of the day, being able to spot elk is a critical skill for consistent success.

It doesn't take a hunter long to realize that if he wants elk, he pretty much has to go into the timber after them. Elk may be out in the open meadows in the morning and evening, when they go there to feed, but for the rest of the daylight hours, they'll be moving through timber toward bedding areas, be resting in their beds in the timber, or be heading back toward the open meadows, again through the timber.

A novice has to train his eye to pick out parts of an elk which are partially hidden by the timber around them. It may be the gleam of the sun off an antler point. It might be the twitch of an elk ear shaking off a fly. Or it might be nothing more than a single eye, staring at you from a tangle of deadfall. There was one morning I can recall, when I saw something that looked like odd-colored sticks that were catching the first rays of light on a faraway slope. I put up the binoculars and found out those odd-colored

There are times when it seems like elk can appear from out of nowhere and can vanish just as quickly. Bob Zellar photo.

sticks were the legs of a herd of eighteen elk. I couldn't pick out the elk themselves without binoculars in that dim light, just saw those sticks that didn't quite fit in. But once I recognized what I saw through those binoculars, the rest of the elk seemed easy to spot, even without the optical help.

As a hunter gains experience, he'll begin to realize that binoculars are a valuable aid no matter where or when he's in elk country. The first place they're used is always out in the open to look at things far away. Then, they become useful in low light situations at dawn and dusk, to gather light and penetrate the distant shadows. But as time goes by, they'll be used more frequently in short-range situations in the timber as well. It's easier to identify an elk part some distance away if you use binoculars. It also forces you to concentrate your sight on one small area and really look it over well. Finally, when you spot an elk in the timber, binoculars can help you map out a strategy to get in position for a clear shot by picking out landforms you can use to hide behind in the course of the stalk.

Some of the other lessons of elk hunting for the novice may not come as quickly. It takes time and familiarity with a rifle to be able to snap it to your shoulder and get off a good shot quickly. More hunters than you could ever imagine have jumped a bull in the timber, identified him as the target they wanted, but had him disappear before they could get off a shot. They may be able to catch that elk with their eye, but catching him through the rifle scope is another matter entirely.

It will also take time to sort out the elk trails, identify the feeding areas, pick out the bedding areas and unravel the mysteries of wallows, rubs, licks, and all the places in between. It's one thing to read about these things. It's quite another to spot them and piece them together in the field. These bits of knowledge will be accumulated and fitted into the puzzle as the first miles of hiking in elk country are put behind you.

As to sure cures for elk fever, however, there simply aren't any. While the novice hunter is more prone to catch it, even the experienced hunter can have his bouts of fever when faced with an exceptional animal, a situation that surprises him, or, even worse, one that develops too slowly. That bout of elk fever could come in the form of a monstrous bull that suddenly materializes before a hunter's eyes and calls for quick action or a cow which decides to walk within range ever so slowly and carefully giving the hunter too much time to think.

One important thing to remember is that every elk hunter, whether they're a novice or a veteran, will sometimes make mistakes. The good elk hunter will accept them and learn from them. The bad elk hunter will try to place the blame elsewhere and have little to show from the experience.

As time goes by, however, the mistakes will become more infrequent, the successes more frequent, and the bank of experience that a hunter can draw on more rich in elk hunting situations and strategy.

Elk hunting will never be easy. The beginner will find that out. There's always something else to try and something more to learn.

But given enough time, you might even be able to make good on the dream of so many novice elk hunters the first time they walk into elk country, to just go out there, and get themselves one of them elks.

Old Equipment, Old Methods

The good old days mean many things to the elk hunter, but comfort certainly wasn't one of them. In fact, today's hunters are rather soft in comparison to how hard the old-timers had to be. And, once you hear about the way it was, it's doubtful that many beginning elk hunters would even want to join the ranks of the hunters of years gone by.

For one thing, elk hunters in the good old days wouldn't think of taking up their rifle until there was snow on the ground and elk country had a good, strong dose of severe winter cold. If the elk weren't moving toward their wintering grounds, or weren't on the wintering grounds already, then it wasn't time to hunt elk. Forget about early season tactics. Forget about that nap you took in the warm autumn sun. These are winter hunting conditions we're talking about. A hunter had his choice of cold, very cold, and subzero cold, and snow, deep snow, and even deeper snow.

It wasn't that the hunters of the good old days were necessarily tougher than those of today. There are some tough hunters today, too. But their life was more primitive. Not only wasn't there a remote unit to operate the TV and VCR so you had to get out of your easy chair, there wasn't even a TV or VCR to show your elk videos and get yourself in the mood for your hunting trip. Talk about tough times!

In terms of the elk hunting itself, it was a similar matter of more primitive technology that set them apart from hunters of today. Their hunting methods and the tools available made them hunt in a particular way that the beginner of today would look at as the difficult way to go about filling the freezer with elk meat.

You should understand, for example, that horses were something outfitters used. The common hunter just didn't have them or the money to rent them. So hunting was done almost totally on foot. Because hunting was done on foot, you had to drag your elk back to the road or pack your elk out on your back. Most hunters chose to drag their elk, making hunts far in the backcountry a poor deci-

In the past, winter's snow provided the best medium to help hunters skid out the elk that they shot. Mark Henckel photo.

sion. That's one of the reasons elk hunters waited until late in the season before heading for elk country. Even on the hunts closer to the end of the road, snow was the medium needed to get those elk back to civilization with the least amount of difficulty.

Drag trails, the hard-packed paths on which elk had been dragged back to the end of the road by others, became the travel networks that hunters used to get around in the old days. These drag trails would thaw and freeze into hard-packed highways to take hunters in to the hunting area early in the morning. Then, they'd make for easy sliding to get your elk back to the vehicle when your hunting was done.

If you wanted to venture off the drag trail into the deep, soft snow, hunters invariably used snowshoes. At that time, any reputable store that handled hunting goods had some snowshoes hanging on the wall. They were basic transportation to get to the elk, and most serious elk hunters had them. They weren't the fastest mode of travel around. Frankly, walking in snowshoes is a lot of work. But it beat wallowing in thigh-deep snow, and if that is what it took to get to the elk, a hunter wore them. These days, snowshoes are not only hard to find, they're also seldom

Horses are the easiest way to pack out elk today, lashing a quarter or a half to the saddle. Mark Henckel photo.

worn even by hunters who have them. For whatever the reason, if the snow is deep enough for snowshoes, the hunter either gets his hands on a horse, uses a snowmobile where legal, or simply doesn't go hunting.

But just because a hunter was tied to his snowshoes didn't mean he was immobile. In deep snow conditions, it was possible for a hunter on snowshoes to literally outrun an elk. He was as good as his ability to handle the snowshoes and when you used them all the time, most serious elk hunters were very good indeed.

Snow in elk country had other benefits for the hunter, too. Its biggest asset, of course, was the ability to read the legacy of tracks the elk left behind and to track the elk themselves. In years of low elk numbers or in areas of low elk density, the hunter who cut a set of tracks would stick with it as long as necessary to catch up to the animal that made it. The hunter who chose not to track was very likely making the decision to have his tag go unfilled.

This combination of deep snow, snowshoes, and elk tracking did mean a hunter had to show a little restraint in his zeal to fill a tag. I can remember following tracks in hunts with my dad where we left the drag trail, donned the snowshoes, and traveled far from the beaten path to see where the sign would lead. Sometimes, when we finally did catch up, Dad would simply tell me not to shoot. By that time, we had gone so far, that getting the animal out was all but impossible. When I asked him why we had tracked the animal that far if we weren't going to shoot it, he answered that it was just to learn what the elk could teach us, to make us better hunters for the animals we could shoot, in places closer to the drag trail.

The elk that were taken within reach of the road would often be dragged by groups of hunters, using much the same system as a hunter using a horse these days. In the old days, a big elk might have four or five men pulling it with ropes. An animal in a tough spot, with a steep climb ahead, might have four or five men hooked to a single quarter to get it to the drag trails. But once you reached the drag trail, the going was relatively easy. It could also be fun. An icy drag trail surrounded by deep snow turned into something akin to a bobsled track with the elk being the sled. Many a kid in elk country, or men who thought they were kids, would sit astride that elk, pull back on its nose to keep it clear of the trail, and have the ride of their lives down the steep, slippery track. They would literally ride their elk out of the mountains with a whoop and a holler.

The hunting methods used weren't the only things that made hunters different in the old days. Their equipment was also far different than what a hunter uses today. The wonder fiber in clothing back then was pure wool. The standard color was red.

Starting with scratchy wool underwear, adding wool shirts and pants, and topping it off with wool caps and coats, the best-dressed hunters relied on high quality wools to keep out the snow and cold. The less-affluent common man of the elk woods was more likely to mix his wools with layers of plain cotton or garments filled with cotton batting to stay as warm as possible. Compare these with the space age fabrics available today and you'll find that hunters of years past fought weight and bulk much more than the elk hunters of today. Today, the watchwords are thin and light. Then, it was thickness and the amount of itching that determined the warmth of the hunter.

To keep hands warm, the standard of days gone by was a pair of leather chopper mittens with a wool mitten liner. Of all the gear in use in days past versus today, these mittens have held up best of all. They're still hard to beat when the mercury crowds the bottom of the thermometer. If there is an improvement today, it's that a hunter is more likely to take a lighter pair of gloves or mittens in addition to his choppers for the times when extreme warmth isn't necessary.

On the other hand, the biggest changes have come in footwear. Insulated boots were unheard of in times long ago. Every hunter, it seemed, relied on some type of overshoe instead, whether it was the type that just went over normal shoes or the much warmer felt shoes that were the top-of-the-line cold weather gear at the time. These overshoes would be worn by hunters on foot or horseback alike. But with the wide variety of boots available today, overshoes are a thing of the past.

The final piece of clothing for the well-dressed elk hunter of long ago was a scarf. Often made of silk, these would keep the wind off the back of a hunter's neck or could be pulled up over his face to prevent the nose and cheeks from freezing in extreme weather conditions. It seems the only ones wearing silk scarves today are the outfitters who wear them as much for decoration as for function. They've been replaced by the hooded coat or the hooded sweatshirt in all but a few rare instances.

One more difference between the elk hunter of today and long ago is the use of fanny packs or day packs by the modern hunter. In older times, a pocket on the back of your hunting coat carried the few things you needed. A rope was tied around your waist to help in dressing and dragging. And a light lunch was simply jammed into the corner of a pocket somewhere in your coat.

The notion of traveling light in those days often meant you left key pieces of equipment behind because your clothing was heavy enough all by itself and your mode of travel over the snow made any additional weight a misery. In hunting with my dad, for example, we'd go the whole day on the scantest of provisions. A sandwich, perhaps an apple, then hunt from before dawn until after dusk. The way he put it, a hungry dog hunts better. And by day's end, I can assure you that this young dog was really hungry.

The elk hunters of decades ago hunted this way because it worked for them. Their clothes were the best available at the time. Their methods were ones that fit the technology of snowshoes, two-wheel drive cars or trucks, and a time that relied more on manpower to get the job done than four-legged or four-wheel-drive

In the past, some elk were even trained to be pack animals like these that are ready to hit the trail. Dick Herriford photo

horsepower.

The thing to remember is that they reflect a time past. While those things may still work in elk country, the beginning hunter shouldn't feel he has to dwell on them for more than a historic look at, or a nostalgic approach to, the sport in which he is embarking. The modern elk hunter has other ways to get the job done more closely attuned to the technology of today and the bank of knowledge available about the animals themselves and how to take them.

To do it totally the old way, I'm afraid, is to do it the hard way. And there's no point in making things any more difficult than they have to be.

Got My Rifle, Ready to Go!

The elk hunter of today is better equipped, better armed, and more knowledgeable about the animal he's seeking than at any time in hunting history. The elk population he's hunting is more widespread, more numerous, and better managed than at any time in hunting history. But is today's hunter more successful in bagging elk than elk hunters were years ago? That all depends. Some are. Some aren't. And the difference is often up to the hunter himself.

As we explored the old days, we found that the world of the elk hunter has changed quite a bit over the years. What we haven't explained so far is that the more successful hunters throughout history have changed with the times.

In elk hunting earlier in this century, hunters were able to take advantage of things like the onset of winter to let the elk come to them. The seasons ran longer in many areas, taking full advantage of the migration to the winter range. Once the elk arrived there, they were under attack from hunter's guns.

Hunters used the technology they had to get their elk. They chained up the old two-wheel drives. They walked the drag trails. They donned snowshoes. And the everyday hunter got after the cows while the few trophy hunters to be found had a heyday in a land of untouched bull populations.

But in the weeks and months before that, the elk were pretty much left alone in the places where they spent the summer and fall. Hunters, for the most part, didn't go after them then because they didn't really have a way to get to them. Or, if they got them, they didn't have a way to get the elk out. The hunters chased deer and birds and anything else earlier in the hunting season. But not elk. Not until the snowflakes came down in earnest and stacked up deep in elk country.

In this way, the elk had a chance for a peaceful existence throughout much of the fall and early winter. They also had areas far back from the roads where they could find security cover away from hunters' guns without much difficulty.

All that has been changed with the technology available and the relative affluence of today's hunters. Hunters in four-wheel drives go to places that the old-timers in two-wheel drives could only dream about. Dudes on horses, whether guided or unguided, are taking to the mountain trails in increasing numbers every year. And snowmobiles glide over the snow far beyond the places a hunter in snowshoes could go. Backpacking gear is lighter. Boots

Throughout history, elk hunters have outfitted themselves with the most modern equipment available. Mark Henckel photo.

No elk is so far into the backcountry that it is beyond the reach of the hunters of today. Michael H. Francis photo.

are more comfortable. Binoculars and spotting scopes are crisper and clearer. Guns are more deadly. Hunters are more knowledgeable about elk. Pick a category, any category, and it almost always comes out the same. Hunters are better able to put pressure on the elk today than at any time in the past.

Then add in one more important factor, the number of hunters. Today, elk are a hot item. Few hunters in states that have elk populations haven't picked up a gun and chased them at some time or another in their hunting career. Hunters elsewhere also feel the tug of the wily wapiti. Those huge antlers seem to cast a spell over almost anyone who has ever leafed through the pages of an outdoor magazine, no matter where they live. Then there's the prospect of putting several hundred pounds of meat in the freezer. That adds up to a pile of pheasant, grouse, rabbit, or even deer dinners.

As a result of the changes in hunting technology, the amount of money that hunters are willing to spend on that technology, and the sheer number of elk hunters that take to the woods every fall, elk are being hunted at times and in places that they've never felt hunting pressure before. There are few pieces of ground, in fact, that haven't felt the step of a hunter's boot if an elk has walked there as well. Elk are being hunted everywhere, by almost everybody, whenever there's a season to legally hunt them.

Despite this pressure, elk have thrived in recent times. The science of game management has seen to that. Fueled by hunters' dollars, wildlife managers have made the moves necessary to expand the range of elk into places that hadn't seen a bull or cow for decades. These elk have repopulated old areas and pioneered new ones. And the same wildlife managers have given us ample opportunity to try the technological advances of today.

So why doesn't every hunter have a full tag by season's end if there are all these elk and the better ways to take them? Hunter numbers is one thing. There simply couldn't be enough elk produced to make everyone a winner at the elk hunting game. But the other reason is that the elk have changed, too.

To survive, they've had to be more secretive. In many areas, they've simply moved further back into places that offer more security from the scourge of hunter's guns. Migration paths have changed and the big bulls seem more reluctant to take them, no matter how deep the snow is they have to buck. Elk vulnerable in bugling time seem to be bugling less. And the animals have relied more heavily on their ability to detect a hunter's presence and quickly put plenty of real estate between themselves and the hunter's gun.

If there ever was such a thing as an easy elk, it is a far rarer commodity now than it was in the past. With the popularity of elk hunting still far from its peak, it will be even harder to come by in the future.

The answer for hunters of today is not to despair over the situation. There's still some elk out there with your tag number on them. But you're less likely to find them if you, too, don't adapt to the changes in time. For the consistently successful elk hunters, that means taking advantage of the gains in technology that have come about over the years and making the most of the opportunities this technology offers you.

This approach is really nothing new. After all, the two-wheel drive replaced the old horse and wagon to get to hunting country. And if we shot at elk with a bow and arrow at anytime in the past century, it was a shot we took by choice rather than necessity. This move to higher technology can be illustrated easily by our choice of firearms for elk. Even in the old days, good hunters used the best they could get their hands on.

This move to the most up-to-date equipment available certainly wasn't lost on my father when he armed himself with the hottest hunting gun of his time, a .250-3000 Savage, in the first decades of this century. This caliber, though it only threw an eighty-seven- or one-hundred-grain bullet, was a veritable killing machine and among the flattest shooting rounds of its time. And my dad knew how to handle it well.

Among his circle of friends and acquaintances, Dad was known as an exceptional hand with a rifle, able to shoot grouse on the wing and place his shots at deer and elk with pinpoint accuracy. I can recall one of my earlier hunting trips with him when we joined the string of cars heading toward Niggerhead Mountain, northeast of Gardiner. When we got there, a bunch of elk was strung out far up the distant mountain, so far in fact, that the hunters gathered below hadn't even pointed a gun at them. I asked Dad why he wasn't shooting. He said because even if we killed one, somebody else would beat us to the elk and put their tag on it. Just to prove it, he showed me.

I've gone back to that spot often and looked up the mountain toward the string of elk he shot at. It was a long, long shot, one I wouldn't take today even with a good scoped rifle. But he pointed his old .250-3000 up the slope, looked over his buckhorn sight, and told me to watch the fourth cow back in the string. He touched off a round and the fourth elk humped up, fell over, and tumbled down the hill. Almost as if it was the shot of a starter's gun, the charge up the hill by the other hunters began, and a barrage of other shots rang out. No one hit another elk. And, just as he said, someone else beat us to the elk with their tag. That didn't make him mad. It was the way elk hunting was at the time. But he proved his point.

Another time, Dad and his .250-3000 made another fine showing when he and his brother-in-law got into some cows. This time, it was late enough in the season that the snow was very deep. At the sight of the elk, my dad pulled up his gun and shot. The cow he aimed at stopped, but didn't fall. He shot again. And again. And again. After four shots, and with the elk not moving, he was beginning to wonder what was going on. As he moved closer, he found that the snow was so deep that the elk couldn't fall, but was just standing there dead on its feet. The brother-in-law later told me that you could have covered all four shots with a silver dollar and they were all through the heart.

In this day and age, and with a relative to talk about, telling someone about this kind of shooting sounds a little like a good old days story that's too good to be true. That's especially true when you consider the elk killing was done with a little eighty-seven grain bullet. Most hunters today wouldn't think of packing anything that light and going after game as large as an elk.

But it taught me early on that it wasn't the size of the caliber that meant as much as what you did with it. In my dad's case, he simply found a round that performed well, a bullet that mushroomed well, and let the bullet placement do the rest. In my formative years as a hunter, it taught me time and time again that bullet placement was the real key to success in bringing down an animal. On the other hand, you could shoot a cannon and if the cannon ball placement wasn't right, the elk would still get away.

When Dad gave up elk hunting, the .250-3000 became my gun and I proved his theory with my own hunting. I can't say how many elk fell to that gun over the years, but its toll was considerable. When it finally began to show its age, I replaced it with a .270 and loads made up with 130-grain bullets. This combination, too, has been disdained by many experts as being too small and too light for an animal the size of an elk. But this gun has also taken its toll of elk, bighorn sheep, deer, bear, antelope, dall sheep, stone sheep, and moose over the years.

The long list of animals taken with that .270 should tell you something about the gun and its shooter. The gun and load is capable. I've shot it long enough that I know that gun and what it will do. And for the novice or veteran elk hunter, this knowledge is going to take you a long way toward putting a tag on an animal.

In my own mind, I've always been an advocate of being a one-gun hunter. To bounce back and forth from gun to gun is to not know any of them well enough to take a good, quick shot under hunting conditions. But if you know that one gun well, it will consistently deliver when you need it most.

Just to make the gun a little more versatile, I've had it fitted with a 3x9 variable power scope. The three-power setting allows me to get a wide view of the target area for hunting in timber. The nine-power option is the reach I need for those long shots

Today's elk hunter has rifle calibers available that can send a bullet over long distances with deadly accuracy. Michael H. Francis photo.

out in the open. The perfect in-between for the user of the fixed power scope is the four-power.

The only risk you run with a variable scope is to forget to turn that power down when you move from the wide-open spaces into the timber. But this problem is usually limited to hunters who use their scope as a replacement for binoculars. And that, to me, is a big mistake in the first place. For one thing, you can't see as well with a scope as you can with binoculars. Even worse, you may find yourself looking over an object that turns out to be another hunter. That means you're pointing your rifle dead at them which is no good under any conditions. Believe me, there's no spookier feeling than to glass a faraway hunter and find out he's looking back at you through his scope.

The combination of .270, 130-grain bullet, and 3x9 scope has proven to be a good one for me. Each year, I sight it in the same, so it hits dead on at twenty-five yards, is three inches high at a hundred yards, dead on at two-hundred seventy-five yards, and is two inches low at three-hundred yards. Being on at twenty-five yards allows me to make head shots on grouse for camp dinner. Being just two inches low at three-hundred yards allows me to hold on the vitals on an elk at that range. And everywhere in between, I know within inches of where that bullet will hit. I've shot it so long that way that I can also tell where the bullet will be on those shots over three-hundred yards.

When the bullet hits the mark, I also know it will mushroom to full potential. Some hunters, when they envision shooting at elk, look at the size of the animal and feel they need special jacketing to hold the bullet together. It's been my experience that most bullet problems come when a hunter worries too much about the bullet holding together or loads his cartridges so hot that they literally explode on impact.

One friend who used one of those deep penetration bullets got a stern lesson from a spike bull he took with a single shot a few years ago. It's true, he got the elk. But the shot he took was from the rear and the bullet entered the spine and went its full length to the front of the animal. When he dug it out, even after going through all that bone, the bullet had hardly opened at all. On any shot through the heart or lungs, it would have opened a hole only about as big as an arrow. Its shocking power would have been minimal at best.

On the other end of the spectrum, Keith Wheat, another hunting friend, had a fondness for red-hot loads out of his .243. Keith was an excellent shot. But he liked to push his loads close to four-thousand feet-per-second and had so much powder poured in his casings that he actually had to tamp it down in order to seat the bullet. It was a load so hot it was dangerously hot to shoot.

There was a time, long ago, when Keith and I snowshoed into elk country while he was using that load and spotted seven cows further down the drainage. It was back in the days when you shot first and worried about rounding up hunters with other tags later so I held the snowshoes while Keith went on ahead to move on the elk. When he got within range, he drew down with that .243 and shot all seven cows with one round apiece. By the time I got there, six other hunters had shown up and Keith had tagged the seventh elk. What we didn't know until we got that elk home and pulled the hide off was that the impact of that lightning fast bullet hitting the elk in the ribs had bloodshot the animal all up and down its side from one end to the other. Every blood vessel under the skin had ruptured under the blast and while the meat was still edible, I'm sure hitting it that way didn't help the eating quality any.

The .243, too, even with a 100-grain bullet, is considered by many to be too small a caliber for elk. Same with the .257 Roberts and its 117-grain bullet. And the .30-30, with its 170-grain bullet, is considered to be too old and slow and useful at too short a range for elk. Yet all of them have downed their share of elk when in capable hands. It all comes down to knowing the limitations of yourself and your gun and knowing how to put that combination together in a hunting situation.

The hottest numbers for elk hunters today are the 7mm. magnum and the magnum .30 caliber loads. These guns pack heavier bullets that will hit with a wallop on the delivery end of a shot. I've talked to hunters who told me that even near-misses on the vitals will down a big elk. As to their stopping power, I really have no complaints. I can't go against the philosophy of a hard-hitting load for elk. But I have my doubts about these big guns for other hunting applications. They can tear up a deer or antelope something fierce, limiting their use as an all-purpose gun. They can pack enough of a kick to give some shooters a bad case of the flinches, limiting the shooter's own abilities. And despite the claims of the near-miss people, your best bet for downing an elk still comes with one, clean, accurate shot.

The bottom line in this talk about shooting technology and its applications to elk hunting is that you have to be able to shoot the gun well. If you can handle the big magnums with deadly accuracy, you're ahead of the game over the smaller caliber shooters. If you can handle the smaller calibers well, you've got enough gun to get the job done.

If I had to pick the perfect rifle calibers for elk hunting, it would probably be the .270 and the .30-06 for their all-around abilities. With the proper loads, they're flat-shooting, adaptable to other game, pack a punch, and their cartridges are available in every small-town store that handles any ammunition at all. That's bound to spark some arguments among the big-caliber boys, but it's calling it as I see it after years of watching elk hunters perform with them.

For the novice elk hunter, the important thing is to land on some caliber elk rifle, big or small, mount a good scope on it, and learn how to use it. It's that performance with the rifle that's going to spell the difference when you see your first elk through the sights.

Then outfit yourself in the rest of the modern gear available. Forget about the old silk scarf, overshoes, and heavy woolens. Get yourself a hooded sweatshirt, polypropylene underwear, a wool shirt, some good boots, binoculars, and a day pack to carry the extras. Try the space age fibers for lightness and warmth. Experiment with the new backpacking gear that can get you far off the beaten path, even if you carry your camp on your back. And try out some cross-country skis for their ability to do the same thing as the old snowshoes, only better and faster. Study the maps and aerial photographs that the old-timers never had. And read everything about elk and elk hunting that you can.

The right gun, the right kind of equipment, and the right kind of knowledge are important parts of the hunting package of today that can give you a big advantage in coping with the new breed of elk and the new breed of elk hunter that are now roaming the West.

First Elk, First Shot, First Miss

If you want to become a good elk hunter, you have to be

THE ELK HUNTER

something of a dreamer. You have to think elk both in and out of season. You must have a vision of the animals you seek. And, most especially, when you're out hunting, you have to believe elk are hiding behind every tangle, that they're out feeding in every mountain meadow, or that they're bedded down just over the next rise. If you don't believe it and don't keep the dream alive, you simply won't be ready to see elk when they present themselves or be ready to shoot when your big chance finally arrives.

But even with the best of elk hunters, it can be a sport of nightmares. It's tough to hang onto the dream. It's tough enough late on the first day when the fatigue of hunting the ups and downs of the mountains sets in. It's tougher still after several days or even several weeks of looking for antlers with nothing to show for your efforts.

There's simply a lot of country in which elk can be hiding. They could be just over the next rise, far into the next drainage, and anywhere or nowhere in between. Without snow on the ground, it's tough to keep up your enthusiasm without being able to spot tracks. Even with tracks in the snow, there's no guarantee that elk are anywhere nearby. And, frankly, even if the tracks are fresh and the elk were here just minutes ago, these big animals can cover so much ground so quickly that they might be miles away by the time you find the sign they left behind.

Veteran elk hunters know how to keep the dream. But that doesn't mean their faith in that dream hasn't been shattered many times in the past. There was a time, in fact, when I was sure that in order to see elk, you had to give up all hope first. You had to walk a million miles, look over several states' worth of real estate through your binoculars, and literally beat your body and mind into such a sorry condition that you were positive that bull elk didn't exist. After you paid those dues, then you might bump into your bull. It would come at a time you didn't expect it, at a place you wouldn't have thought would hold an elk. Suddenly, an elk would simply materialize, big and broad and there.

When you see elk that way, the first tendency is to chalk it up to luck. But that's not true. It's too much of a coincidence that there are some hunters who are successful every year, some that find success at several-year intervals, and still others who never seem to connect with an elk. Luck can play a role, but not as big a one as you might think.

The sight of a big bull elk has stricken even some veteran hunters with a bad case of elk fever. Bob Zellar photo.

Time is the big difference between the veteran elk hunter and the novice which really does matter. It's not just any old time, however. What we're talking about here is productive time. This poductive time expresses itself in several ways and means several different things to the elk hunter.

Back in my desperation days, I used to think that my time was being wasted if there wasn't an elk in it. I felt that the time in elk country was simply something you put in between elk, much the same way a worker sometimes watches the clock waiting for the payoff that comes at quitting time. While it's true that if you spend enough time in elk country, the payoff will eventually come in the form of blind luck, the parallel between the workplace and elk country can be carried one step further. The worker who uses his time wisely and puts more effort into the job will reap more dividends than one who simply goes through the motions. An elk hunter, too, learns that rewards come for those who use their time wisely.

An observant hunter will pick up valuable pieces of the puzzle even on the days he sees no elk if only he can read the sign the elk left behind. That may be nothing more than finding a hidden pass that elk use when they're pressured. It might be a hidden route to a secluded bench where bulls can bed with a good view of the country below. It could be discoveries of licks, rubs, or wallows. Or it might be just an insight into the lives of the elk themselves.

I never really realized how elk could cruise through the country they call home until just one of those days when I sat on a high point and watched a bunch through binoculars far away. These elk were so far in the distance that there was no way I ever could have caught up with them, so I watched just to see what they would do. The herd didn't look like they were moving hard at all. They were just moving at a steady pace. Yet in the fifteen to twenty minutes that I tracked them, they covered two to three miles. Is it any wonder that elk can be in this drainage today and far away tomorrow. It made me wonder about all the elk I had spooked over the years and had me pondering how far they must have gone. It also answered some questions about how I could hunt an area for several days without seeing any sign only to arrive for another day's hunt and find it loaded with elk.

On another of my many learning days without any close calls with elk, I took to wandering game trails until I cut across an old one that was noticeably wider and cut deeper than any of the rest. The few tracks I found on the trail all led down a steep slope. That wasn't necessarily the direction I wanted to go, but my curiosity got the best of me. I followed the tracks clear to the bottom of a deep basin, where I was rewarded with the discovery of a clear, cold spring bubbling into a little pool. There were old trails fanning out from that spring in all directions. They weren't being used heavily at the time, a fairly wet year. But in a dry autumn in the mountains, that spring just might pay off as a spot to ambush an elk. No matter how dry the year, that spring has bubbled cold and clear. The drier the year, the more elk activity I find around it. The wetter the year, the fewer the elk. Even on a day without elk, it was like finding a jewel.

All alone, these discoveries really don't seem like much. They don't seem like much in comparison to shooting a bull elk on those days, anyway. But it's those types of discoveries that are part of your investment in elk of the future. They help you to learn your

A hunter has to be ready to shoot, because most elk have escape cover just a few steps away. Michael H. Francis photo.

chosen hunting areas on an intimate basis. They help you to make a better guess on where the elk will be and when you can find them there. They'll offer insights into what elk will do when you spook them. And they'll help you to use your time in elk country more wisely, increasing the chances that luck will be on your side in a short time rather than a long time.

This time spent in elk country and the lessons that can be learned there can be helped immeasurably by going there with someone already experienced in the ways of elk. That person can point out the things through their experienced eyes that it might take you years to pick out by yourself.

As we said earlier, probably the best way to learn is as a child growing up in elk country. That gives you the most time to assimilate elk knowledge and to grow with the sport of elk hunting. But there's a word of caution here for the adults who would bring youngsters into the elk hunting world. It wouldn't be fair to say that elk hunting is a man's or a woman's sport, for there are teens out there who do a remarkably good job of it. But there are others who never get a fair chance to develop a liking for the sport simply because of the rigors of elk hunting.

It's possible, for example, in a veteran hunter's zeal for the novice to find success, that they literally burn them out or sour their attitudes toward elk hunting. You can't take twelve or fourteen or sixteen-year-old legs and walk them upslope and downslope all day long, day after day, and week after week. For all the energy teens seem to have, stamina is something that generally comes with more age along with the wisdom to pace yourself.

You can't expect a novice hunter to be immune from elk fever and not miss an easy shot. Lord knows, even veteran elk hunters make horrible misses when they're hit by the fever. I've made my share. You may have, too. In fact, I know of world record holders at the shooting game who shake their heads in amazement over some of the easy shots they've missed over the years.

Whatever they do, veteran elk hunters should make the hunting experience a positive one, giving the novice every courtesy and bit of encouragement they wanted for themselves when they were brand new at the sport. Only the bombastic or the downright mean would give them anything else.

One of the saddest scenes I ever witnessed in elk country came after a young hunter made a less-than-perfect but killing shot on a cow that turned out to be his first elk. Rather than glad-handing, back-patting, chest-thumping praise for that youngster, the teen was ridiculed by a parent who thought he should have done better. All the pride of a first elk was robbed from that boy. All the fun of the hunt was taken away. And, I'm afraid, rekindling the all-important elk hunting dream in that novice hunter would have been just about impossible at that moment.

As far as I'm concerned, making mistakes and learning from them are just a part of being new at anything. If you're both young and new at something, the miscues are all the more predictable. How else could you explain the folly of my own youth when I decided to put my tongue on a gun barrel on a below-zero day to see what would happen and ended up leaving several layers of skin behind when I finally pulled it free. Why did I do it? Darned if I know. It just seemed like the right thing to do at the time. But I can assure you I only did it once. And given the time to mature as an elk hunter, most of the other mistakes of youth will be remedied the same way.

This tolerance toward novices should hold true no matter what the age of the new hunter. The term, "babes in the woods," applies equally to newcomers of all ages. Frankly, many get into the game not knowing what they're really getting into. They don't know much about elk, elk hunting, or elk country. For the veteran hunter who accompanies them, that newness should translate into tolerance and patience in the face of probable mistakes. For the novice, it's a chance to ask plenty of questions and learn from the experience of someone more wise in the ways of elk than they are.

Often, however, the novice becomes embarrassed about how little they know even when the veteran is willing to help. For these hunters, I like to prime the pump, so to speak. I'll ask them why this track is going a certain direction, what they think that elk wallow is for, or when the elk made a certain rub. For the beginners who aren't inquisitive, it gets them thinking about elk and what they do and breaks the ice on the issue of how their inquiries will be received. Soon, they're the ones asking questions as they become more observant of the elk sign they see, hear, and smell around them. And when they reach that point, the novice's time in elk country will begin to become more productive.

The key here is to get the dream started and keep it alive in the novice elk hunter. It's that dream that will carry them along when the going gets tough and desperation starts to take over. It's that dream that will spur them on to become veteran elk hunters themselves instead of someone who just tried it a few times and then put their gun away. And it's that almighty dream which will make the biggest difference in their elk hunting future when they come face-to-face with their first elk, their first shot, and, perish the thought, their first miss. They'll know it's just all part of the game.

Shortcut to an Elk

We've talked here a lot about paying dues, putting in time, and gathering knowledge before a novice can expect to become a consistently successful elk hunter. We haven't talked as much about the shortcut to an elk.

There are some hunters who don't want to spend many days hunting elk, weeks planning their hunt, and years learning about the animals themselves and the country they live in. There are some who are looking for a quick fix and an even quicker shot at a bull. To do that, you're going to have to rely on someone else

A guided hunt often offers clients the most comfortable way of taking the bull elk of their dreams. Mark Henckel photo.

to pay your dues. Then you'll pay them for that knowledge, skill, and experience. This shortcut is hiring an outfitter and making the most of his or her ability in helping you get an elk.

The bulk of this book deals with hunting the other way. It goes into detail on how to get an elk on your own. The reason for that is most hunters choose to hunt elk that way. They either live in elk country and hunt it every year or live far away and make their annual plans to drive there, then camp and hunt on their own.

But outfitters provide a viable alternative for many hunters for many different reasons. Their camps provide comforts that are unattainable in most car camping situations including warm, dry tents, good hot meals, and a measure of help every step of the way. They usually have horses, which makes getting into elk country easier for older hunters, those whose health may be threatened by more strenuous methods, or anyone else that likes an easier entry to the hunting area. They know the country where they're hunting like the back of their hand. They know the places in that country where the elk are likely to be. They know what to do with an elk once it's on the ground. They know how to get the elk and elk hunter back to civilization. In short, a good outfitter can offer you more comfort, more help, and more success than you can usually get on your own.

Of course, you pay for this. And these days, frankly, you pay quite a lot. The price tag alone means this is not the way to go for many elk hunters.

Wayne Hoope, who outfitted in the Gardiner, Montana, area into the 1960s and whose son, Billy, now handles hunters in the area, can remember how the outfitter's price list grew. Back in the 1930s and early '40s, Hoppe helped his father, Paul, when the charge was $6 a day for a guide, horse, room, and board. Even when Hoppe quit the business in 1965, he was only getting $30 a day for the same services.

All that's changed now. Some rough figures on outfitted hunts today would be in the ballpark of $250 to $300 a day per hunter. Start adding up the fees for a standard four, seven, or nine-day hunt and tack the cost of most nonresident licenses on top of that and you can see there's a major monetary investment in filling that elk tag.

It should be pointed out, however, that outfitters are not getting rich at this business. They charge what they do because their operations don't come cheap. The purchase and upkeep of a string of horses or mules all year long is not a low-budget item. There's tack for the stock, tents, stoves, cooking equipment, and other assorted gear. The good outfitters don't skimp on the quantity or quality of the food you eat while in camp. They have to pay their guides, cooks, wranglers, and any of the other support personnel involved in their operation. There are often Forest Service permits to be paid. Camps must be put in before the season and taken out when it's done. Insurance is no longer a low-ticket or optional item. And, finally, there's the outfitter's own piece of the action in order to support himself and his family. Add it all up and figure that hunting seasons aren't available on a year-round basis and you can understand why they charge what they do.

While paying those fees and going on a guided hunt will provide a shortcut to an elk, it is by no means a guarantee. Even the best of outfitters can come up dry when herd numbers are at the low point in their cycle or the weather refuses to cooperate.

What's even more frustrating, however, is when the elk are there but the hunter comes in so ill-prepared, out-of-sorts, or unreasonable that they blow the opportunities that the outfitter provides. That's the time when both the outfitter and the hunter

This Is Elk Hunting

come away from the hunt unfulfilled and often angry over what transpired in the field.

I can remember one classic situation when I was working as a guide for an outfitter friend and had two nonresident hunters some seventeen miles back in the wilderness. I figured things were going our way on our first day out when we spotted three bulls about a quarter of a mile away. We were ready to move in when all hell broke loose. The two guys suddenly couldn't decide who was going to take the first shot. And they got in an argument over it. "I'm going to shoot first," one of them said. "No, I'm going to shoot first," the other replied. Neither hunter would accept a coin flip to decide the issue. Neither would give an inch as the bickering continued there, just a short stalk away from the elk. Finally, I'd had enough. I told them neither of them would shoot, pulled them out of there, and took them back to camp where they were instructed to settle the issue for once and for all. In the meantime, the other guides and I decided to keep those two apart for the rest of the hunt.

It snowed that night, and the following morning, I had one of the hunters in tow when we cut some elk tracks at first light. We followed a single set and then cut up above them, working back down the slope from bench to bench. We finally spotted the source of those tracks, a good six-point bull in its bed, looking down the slope. At that, the hunter looked at me and said, "Should I shoot? Should I shoot?" I'll admit I used a little profound language on him to get him stimulated and then asked how long he expected that bull to wait for him. By then, the bull was up on its feet and starting to move out. The hunter shot and promptly plugged him in the rear end. Four more shots and he finally stopped the bull with a second hit.

To say the hunter got a little excited and stayed that way for the rest of the day would be an understatement. That night, back at camp, he was drying out his clothing near the fire and managed to burn up one mitten, a sock, part of his cap, and one end of his boot. The hunter was in another world all to himself and wasn't thinking too clearly. And, I should add, seventeen miles back in the wilderness is no place to start burning up equipment critical for keeping you warm. I decided then and there that going into the backcountry for elk may be fun, but I didn't want to be an elk guide.

The knowledge of a guide or outfitter can overcome some tall odds in hanging tags on many elk. Bill Hoppe photo.

For every horror story about guiding hunters, however, there is usually another tale which surprises you in a positive way. One of my more pleasant surprises came when I took my cousin Benny, from Pennsylvania, and several of his friends on a similar hunt. Like the other hunters, we packed back into the wilderness and set up camp. And, just like the others, we got lucky on our first day out, spotting an elk just at daylight. This elk was moving through patches of timber a distance away, so I told my cousin to watch him and shoot if it proved to be a bull. The shot was far from an easy one, at a moving elk some three-hundred to four-hundred yards away. When the elk finally stepped into an opening, he said it was a bull, but instead of using the log that was there for a rest, my cousin threw up the gun and took an offhand shot. To my surprise, the elk went down.

It turned out that Benny and his friends were avid whitetail hunters, well accustomed to taking offhand shots at running deer. But it sure startled me he was that good a shot. The elk he took was a four-by-five bull which might as well have been an eight-point. It was certainly a trophy to him.

When we got back to camp, we found out that another in the group had jumped a six-point bull at noon, shot it, dressed it out, and then came back to camp to report the news. It was quite a celebration, but the other hunter was a little worried about having to leave that bull back in the timber until the following day when we would go back in with horses and pack it out. He was afraid something would happen to it.

My brother Doug and Benny took off toward the elk the following morning while his friend and I led the horses in by a longer route. On the way in, I'll admit I had a little fun with him. I told him he should have covered it with branches to keep the animals away and to hide it from other hunters. I told him guys with helicopters sometimes came through and if they spotted an elk on the ground, they would land and carry it off. By the time we got to the kill site, the man was really agitated. He became more so when we arrived and found the elk gone with only a hand-written note left behind on the entrails that read, "Thanks for the elk — The Coyote Gang."

The hunter broke down then and there. He was forty-five or fifty years old, but he was crying like a baby. Even I got to feeling bad for him, despite the fact I could see the skid trail in the snow where the elk had been pulled over the hill. As I correctly figured, Doug and Benny had gotten there first and pulled the elk over the hill and out in the open so we could load it easier. Then they left the note, just for fun.

When I told the hunter where his elk was, the man did a complete turnaround. He went from tears of sorrow to tears of joy in an instant. In the end, the story had a happy ending. The man had the six-point mounted and the Coyote Gang's card framed and both still hang in his home back in Pennsylvania.

The two elk taken on the first day of their Montana hunt turned out to be the only ones bagged that trip by the group, despite seven more days of hunting the backcountry. That only proves the adage that sometimes you score on the first day, sometimes on the last day, and sometimes you don't score at all.

For the nonresident hunter, this means you would be well advised to make the most of your opportunities when you get them and to appreciate the elk you have on the ground. There is nothing more frustrating for a guide or outfitter nor more disrespectful to the elk themselves than to hear a hunter start complaining about an animal they've shot once it's on the ground. Too often if it's a smaller bull, a four-point or a five-point, or perhaps if it has a tine broken off its antlers, the hunter gets angry or upset and starts bitching that it wasn't really big enough.

If they pulled the trigger on it, it must have been big enough when they looked through their sights. If it wasn't, they shouldn't have pulled the trigger.

In all honesty, hanging your tag on any bull elk is nothing to sneeze at. Once you've chased them long enough, you'll realize that every bull is somebody's trophy. Once you've chased them long enough, you'll also realize that few elk are gifts. Most of them are earned. And you owe the animals themselves the respect of appreciating what the elk world gives you rather than worrying over what might have been.

As far as making yourself and your outfitter happy, probably the single most-important factor is to be ready for the chances that are presented to you. That means being familiar with your gun before you get into a hunting situation. After a hunter misses a shot or two at an elk is no time for the outfitter to discover that the gun wasn't sighted in or was sighted in last year and wasn't checked since. The best way to prepare is to shoot it often enough to be familiar with it before you arrive in hunting country and then to check it once again to make sure your travels haven't knocked the sights off line.

Another factor is to give yourself enough time to be able to hunt effectively and have a real chance for success. If it takes a day or two for your body to adjust to the high elevations of elk country, your chances for success on a four-day elk hunt are slim indeed. If your leg joints are so beat and battered by the ride in on horseback that you can't move the next day, your hunting effectiveness will also be diminished. And if you don't know anything about elk and how to hunt them, you're going to be spending all your hunting time learning the basics instead of taking advantage of the advanced course that an outfitter can provide.

It's true that an outfitter can provide a shortcut to getting an elk. A novice will be better equipped, better cared for, more effective, and have a better chance for success than he ever could hope for on his own. But even in an outfitted situation, the time in days and the time in years can't help but make them a more consistently

A hunter looking for an outfitter should find out exactly what that outfitter's camp has in terms of equipment. Don Laubach photo.

successful elk hunter. In that way, the dues still have to be paid by somebody, whether it's the novices themselves or the guides that accompany them. Someone has to put in the time, walk the many miles, make the mistakes, and do their homework on elk.

To move on to the next stage in elk hunting, that of the elk hunter who begins to find success on a regular basis on his own and understands the reasons why, you have to begin gathering more pieces of the puzzle. And, I'm afraid, the only way to do that is by paying more dues.

■

THESE ARE ELK

It doesn't take an elk hunter long to realize that if you're going to hunt elk, you've got to know something about them. It's just not enough to know that they're real big critters that live in the mountains.

The task of learning all about elk isn't as simple as it seems. There's much to learn. And once you learn it, you have to apply that knowledge to the elk country at hand.

You can't go after record book bulls until you know what it takes for an elk to make the record book. You have to be able to pass judgement on the elk you see. You also have to know that the area you plan to hunt has record book bulls in it.

Just as the novice learned that all elk country isn't created equal when it comes to holding elk, the hunter at this level of development has to learn that all elk hunting spots within it aren't created equal either. You have to do your homework and ask the right questions to make sure you are hunting in the right spot. You have to be able to read maps and know the type of country that you're looking for. And you have to make conscious decisions on exactly the place you plan to hunt.

In many ways, the elk hunter may feel that he's still at the research stage. What he has to understand is that as long as he hunts and the more successful he becomes, the more that research will play a critical role in that success.

The mistake of newcomers to the elk hunting game is that they often blunder around aimlessly in elk country. By now, the elk hunter knows that planning plays an important part in his hunting success. He's learning more and more about the animal that he's seeking. And he not only is picking up more pieces of the elk hunting puzzle, but he's learning how they fit together.

Of all the stages of an elk hunter's personal development, these times are perhaps the most important. Anyone can get lucky and pick up an elk from time to time. But to make your own luck and to find it year in and year out, you have to keep paying those dues.

What Are We Hunting Anyway?

Paying your dues in elk country means more than just taking a few strolls through the autumn mountains. You've got to work at learning about elk in the days, weeks, and years you spend on their home turf. That knowledge begins with knowing what an elk looks like.

It almost seems too simple. We all know what elk look like, right? We've seen the mounted heads and the pictures in the outdoor magazines and we may even have seen some face-to-face. They're sort of brownish-colored critters with long legs and a rectangular body and big antlers. The trouble is that these characteristics roughly cover a lot of different animals. They especially cover them if you're looking at an animal through a tangle of timber, on a faraway mountainside, or in the dim light of morning and evening. Your eyes will fool you if you don't look close and know exactly what you're looking for.

More than a few moose have been plugged by hunters under those circumstances. There are enough of them that die every year in certain parts of Montana, for example, that the illegal kill has cut into the number of permits awarded to hunters to take them legally during the hunting season.

There are more than a few hunters who have pulled off long and difficult stalks during low light periods of the day, only to sneak up on a bunch of mule deer instead of an elk. Judging the difference between the size of a deer and the size of an elk at a

There are times when it seems like elk use mirrors to befuddle the hunters trying to draw a bead on one. Bob Zellar photo.

distance can be difficult.

Then there's the story that Doris Whithorn, of Livingston, Montana, tells of a hunter in the old, steam train days who shot a mule, realized his mistake, and left it lay far back in the mountains. Unfortunately, his friends knew he shot the mule and they knew where. So they went back in, dressed it out, dragged it out, and loaded it on the train to be delivered to the hunter back in town, metal shoes on its feet and all.

Or, how about the other tale from the Gardiner area about the hunter who was riding on a buckskin-colored horse while following elk tracks. When he thought he was close to the elk, he tied up his horse in the timber and continued on foot. But the elk fooled him and made a big circle before heading off in a different direction. The hunter, trying to save himself some walking, decided to take a shortcut back to his horse. He was taking this shortcut when he saw the tell-tale color of elk hide ahead of him and shot, killing his own horse.

Another horse tale involved a youngster who didn't just shoot a horse, he shot it right out from under another hunter who was riding it at the time.

The common denominator among all these hunters was that they knew what an elk looked like. They were sure of it. Without question. No hesitation. Consider the elk tag filled. Yet there was a breakdown somewhere between the elk identification and the pulling of a trigger that resulted in an embarrassing situation in which another kind of animal was either killed or nearly killed by mistake.

The truth of the matter is that you have to know elk on a relatively intimate basis to be able to pick them out under any conditions and know what you're seeing. You have to know what to look for to make a positive identification that will stand up when you spot an animal in circumstances less desirable than the front page of an outdoor magazine.

An easy place to start is to consider the name wapiti, an Indian word for elk. Wapiti, literally translated, means white deer. It's easy enough to figure out how elk could get such a name. Bulls, especially old bulls and most especially old bulls on the winter range, look almost white in their thick coats.

Elk color varies by sex and age. Cows tend to be a more even shade and darker brown than the bulls, which often have a buckskin color. Younger bulls are darker in color than older bulls. Bulls have a rich color on their undersides, a deep chestnut brown, which is even darker in color than cows and stands in marked contrast to the lighter-colored hair on the upper parts of their bodies.

By being able to distinguish between the colors and where they're found on an elk, it's possible to make a pretty good guess at what you're looking at through a spotting scope, even in poor light and even at a distance. If you bump into a bunch of elk with that characteristic light buckskin color, it's a fair bet you're looking at a bunch of bulls. From there, you can get a gauge on what to hang your tag on by looking at the color again.

If you're looking for a good-eating bull, look for the darker animals. Bulls with dark, shiny coats are likely to be the younger animals and thus, the better eating. If you're looking for a bull to hang on the wall, look for those white deer in the group with the light-colored coats. You shouldn't pull the trigger, of course, until you get a look at the headgear they're sporting. That's still

A hunter can often tell the oldest bull in a group by the sagging belly that shows their older age. Michael H. Francis photo.

the best way to be sure of your target and be sure you're shooting an animal that's within the limits of the law. But using color as a key will at least give you a start in knowing where to look.

Compared to the buckskin and brown colors of an elk, mule deer are much more gray as they head into the fall. By winter range time, they're all gray. Moose range from dark brown to almost black and have that bulbous nose and palmated antlers to set them apart. Horses and mules sometimes have pack saddles, riding saddles, bridles, and lead ropes on them, unlike any of the above, and there's nothing in the wild that has anything like their long and distinctive tail. To make a positive identification on any of these animals, force yourself to pay attention to the details to make sure of your target.

Taking note of body shape and size will also provide a key to help you in identifying and aging your bull. Like many an elk hunter as they get older, an elk's chest will tend to slide into his belly. That more protruding belly line can provide a good clue to an older bull. It could also mean that the elk have had a great year with plenty of feed, but, once again, it's a tendency to consider when looking over a bunch of bulls.

The muzzle and head of an old bull also tends to look more massive than that of a younger animal, which has sleeker lines.

These Are Elk

A hunter must look at all the clues that different elk provide, then verify his target by looking for antlers. Bob Zellar photo.

All these things are minor details, but they add up to a lot of pieces of the puzzle when looking over a single elk or trying to pick out an individual among a group of elk. Looking for details, in fact, will probably tell you more about the animals in front of you than simply trying to make your decision on body size alone. It's true that bulls are bigger than cows are bigger than calves. But much of the difference in size depends on the age and nutrition of the animal. And there is plenty of overlap between the sexes.

Mature bulls may run from seven hundred to one thousand pounds on the hoof for an exceptional animal. Cows will generally run from five hundred to eight hundred pounds. Calves will tip the scales at anywhere from less than a hundred pounds to several hundred pounds depending on the lateness of their birth and the stage of the season you're hunting them.

Hunters who live in elk country have a decided advantage in being able to look over enough elk to tell these differences and spot the tiny details that add up to the elk they're looking for. If you live far away, that kind of living library is simply unavailable. You can pick up what you can during your hunting trips, but this kind of exposure to the animals happens for short periods of time only once a year. The only reasonable alternative to the living library is the library in your hometown. Look through books on the subject and try to pick out the subtle differences between animals. Try to find old copies of the outdoor magazines and do the same. It isn't quite like looking at the real thing, but it's better than nothing at all.

By looking at many elk in whatever situation is available to you, it will help you make a quick identification when you get into the field with a gun in your hands and will help you to pick out and take aim at the elk of your dreams.

How Big Is Big?

When I close my eyes, what I see is a bull elk so big that when he turns his head, he hooks himself in the rear end with his own antlers. I want eyeguards that run the full length of his muzzle before they turn up. And I want antler mass that's so heavy that there's no question in my mind that the bull has record book written all over him.

When you talk about big bulls, that's big. It's big enough that a hunter grabs his rifle a little tighter and squeezes the trigger a little more carefully when he takes a shot. There's good reason for his care, too. It's very likely a shot at the elk of a lifetime.

The name of the game for many hunters today is shooting a big bull. The bigger the better. As we talked about earlier, it wasn't always that way. It used to be cows that were king, while the big old bulls were looked on as nothing more than jerky on the hoof when it came to their eating potential. Trophy hunters today must shake their heads when they think about the good old days. Back then, the few hunters going after bulls had their pick of a lot of fine animals. The biggest bulls were undoubtedly the last to be shot. And when a big bull was downed, his antlers were simply knocked off with an axe and left for rodent feed.

But times change and hunters change with them. These days, hunters are looking for the monster hat rack that a big bull sports on his head. But if your decision is to shoot a good bull, a record book bull, or something in between, you have to be able to recognize one when you see him. You also have to understand the odds you're facing in accomplishing the feat.

Big bulls with a good spread and symmetrical antlers are needed to ensure a good score. Don Laubach photo.

The first thing to realize for the would-be trophy hunter is to not worry about being able to recognize a really huge bull. When you bump into a real monster, there's never any question in your mind as to what's out in front of you. Those big six, seven, and eight-points seem to stand out so much from the crowd that they're unquestionably big.

The problem then becomes one of being able to distinguish just plain big from unquestionably big. You have to be able to evaluate a bull quickly because you may have only a moment or two to make your decision.

When looking at bulls for their trophy potential, there are several main things that you could look for, including the number of points the elk has. An inexperienced hunter usually starts at the eyeguard and just starts counting back on each side until he comes up with the total. But the more experienced elk hunter quickly learns to look for the fourth point and let that be his guide. That fourth point is the longest point and is easily spotted. Then you just have to count how many points he has behind it, whether it's one or two or three.

Once you get the system down, it doesn't take long to size up a bull. You count the points, get a fix on how wide the rack is, and take a look at how heavy the antlers are and you can make your decision on whether or not to pull the trigger in a hurry. I can remember a hunt with my sons Wade and Kirk and nephew Russ after spotting a couple of bulls in the distance on Thanksgiving Day. I asked the kids if they wanted to go after the elk the next day and the verdict was unanimous. We awakened early the next morning and were at the spot we were going to take off from an hour before daylight. Wade and Russ went up one side of the ridge while Kirk, the younger son, and I took the other. Wade and Russ got quite a way ahead of us and made it to the top first. When they got there, they looked down in a canyon and saw a group of seven bulls on the move. Two of them were quickly determined to be the biggest and the boys decided to go after them, taking off at a dead run to cut them off at a place where the elk would have to cross a clearing. The ambush was complete when the elk walked out as if on command and the boys shot the two big bulls.

Wade's bull was the bigger of the two with a beam length of fifty-two inches and an inside spread of forty-eight inches. Russ' bull was just a bit smaller with an inside spread of forty-seven inches and a slightly shorter main beam. Both bulls scored in the three-hundred-sixty to three-hundred-seventy range according to Boone and Crockett Club scoring. That fell short of the minimum to make the record book, but they were fine specimens anyway, certainly fine enough to please the boys that shot them.

The fact the bulls were shot on the day after Thanksgiving is fairly typical of most big bull hunting. It seems the later in the season a hunter is able to wait, the better his chances of shooting a truly big bull. Part of it is the weather conditions, with snow and cold moving the elk down to lower elevations. Part of it is the cold weather alone and the fact the elk have to feed longer and move around more.

A hunter should realize, however, that he can't go just anywhere to shoot a big bull, even if he does wait until the tail end of the season. There are a lot of factors that go into producing a bull of trophy quality and all of them have to be there if you ever hope to bump into a record book animal.

You have to find, for example, an area that has good genetics to produce the animal. Some places never have produced big bulls and they never will. Then, there are the vagaries of abnormal horns that seem to be passed from generation to generation. With the Boone and Crockett requirements putting a premium on a symmetrical set of antlers, those freak points can cost in a big way.

While working on a film with wildlife cinematographer Gordon Eastman, there was a group of six bulls that we called in during the month of February. At the time, only the spike portion of their antlers had grown and the overall length of the spikes was twenty to twenty-four inches. Three of the bulls had abnormal antlers. One had a pedicel, the bony base the antlers grow from, that came out right between its eyes. The other two emerged from over the top of their left eye and had antlers that curved downward. Gordon and I visited the place again the following August and found the same group of elk. One of the abnormal bulls had turned into a six-point on one side with a big blob of antler material on the other. The other two were freak four and five-points.

All the elk in the group had shown amazing growth during that time, but in terms of trophy potential, they were all too badly deformed. Yet the pattern of abnormal antlers like these seem to have been passed from generation to generation. In the Gardiner area, there seems to be some sort of gene passed that affects a certain number of bulls with one freak antler each year. Whether that's being passed along by a dominant bull with that trait is anyone's guess. But it seems to happen often enough that there's more than just the element of chance at work.

The importance of this is that a hunter who hopes to shoot a big wall-hanger or an elk for the books can't afford to get caught with an animal with freak antlers. Or, he can't take an animal with broken antlers. Or, he can't take an animal that is anything short of perfect. With only a limited amount of time to look over elk before taking a shot, often it isn't easy to pick out the abnormalities.

Wade had a late permit one year where just that kind of thing happened to him. We had spotted a bunch of elk the night before and by first light the following morning, we were up above their feeding area, looking down on them. One of the bulls was a nice six-point. But another looked to have an exceptional spread. It was so much wider than the others that it had to be a trophy. But,

Sometimes bulls will break off an entire antler, and if you get only a side profile before you shoot, you'll be sadly surprised. Michael H. Francis photo

as often happens, things began to take place in a hurry. The elk started to move and I coached Wade to shoot at the bull with the wide spread. The elk did turn out to be a dandy. It had an inside spread of fifty-two inches with heavy six-point antler on one side. But on the other, the fifth point was missing. It had been broken off.

If you're shooting a bull for its trophy score, you've got to make sure it has all its points. If not, the deductions will kill you. There have been some tremendous bulls taken in the West that came up short of the magic qualifying scores for state record books, Safari Club International recognition, Boone and Crockett, or Pope and Young honors just because they were missing a point.

A trophy elk also has to have some help from nature to reach that status. He has to have good feed and ample water. There have to be minerals in the grass he eats or in the licks he visits that can help his antlers grow long, heavy, and strong. If they don't, they'll be splintered or broken off in the mock fights of the pre-rutting period or the battles of the breeding season. And, probably most important of all in this day and age, a bull has to be able to grow old to grow big.

Of all the variables that go into producing a trophy bull elk, none are as critical today as the age of the animal. Most areas that the public can hunt receive heavy pressure during the archery, rifle, and black powder seasons available. As a result, even the bulls who have all the other ingredients for big antlers going for them, never get a chance to produce a trophy head. They're killed before they can reach the eight, nine, or ten years of age that it takes to fully mature. Before that time, they may have the number of antler points. They may have the length and spread. But they won't have the heavy mass that it takes to get into the books.

This problem of hunting pressure puts the would-be trophy hunter in quite a dilemma. It's easiest to get access and a license to hunt areas where plenty of other hunters have done the same thing. But the big bulls these days are often coming from areas that have put some kind of restrictions on the ability of hunters to pursue elk there. Some states have gone to point restrictions on the elk. You can't shoot less than a branch-antlered bull. Perhaps you can't shoot less than a four-point bull. Or, best of all for the trophy hunters, you have to have a special permit to hunt a certain area.

If the third antler point is too small, it will cost a hunter dearly. Michael H. Francis photo.

These Are Elk ▪

73

Limiting the number of hunters by the number of permits that are issued is something of a double-edged sword for an elk hunter. It can give the elk enough protection that they get old enough to produce a trophy-size set of antlers. Sooner or later, we'll see more trophy bulls in the record books because of it. But these permit areas also limit the opportunities of hunters. Not everyone has a chance to hunt there. Some hunters, in fact, may wait years between permits. And if you truly love to hunt elk, that kind of waiting game really hurts.

All a hunter can hope for is to make the most of the opportunities he has and recognize the bull he wants when he sees him. For a record book bull, that means some impressive measurements from one end of the rack to the other. The main beam needs to be pretty close to fifty-five inches long. The inside spread can't afford to be less than forty-five inches. Perfect would be fifty-five. The eyeguards, second-points, and third-points should all be eighteen to twenty or more inches long. The fourth point should be twenty-four or more inches long. And even the fifth and sixth points should be at least a foot long. Then, the overall mass of the antlers has to be good. The first measurement, taken at the narrowest point between the eyeguard and the second point, should be twelve inches in circumference.

A bull that big looks huge from any angle. With a fifty-five-inch main beam, that puts the tip of its antlers clear back by its rump when the bull puts its head back. The higher and the more they sweep back, the bigger the bull.

But there are pitfalls all along the way in getting a bull with those kinds of measurements. Many a bull has long points up and down the rack, except for a short third point. That, in itself, is enough to keep it out of the book. Perhaps the fifth and sixth points are short. That, too, will keep it out.

Believe it or not, some hunters will take a bull that falls into the trophy class as the first elk they shoot. Then they'll spend the rest of their hunting life trying to match the feat. Even the most experienced of hunters rarely are lucky enough to shoot a big bull every year, much less a record book bull. It's a fact of hunting life that these bulls should be treated like rare treasures because there are so few of them around.

The important thing is to set your goals and decide how big is big for you while remembering that beauty is in the eye of the beholder. One man's trophy may be another man's runt. Remember too, that you've got your work cut out for you if you want to be a trophy hunter.

If a hunter is willing to settle for something less and perhaps find success with more regularity, he should be ready for that, too, and still thank his lucky stars if a trophy bull happens his way.

No matter their size, each bull you see and each you pull the trigger on will add a few more memories to your lifetime of hunting experiences. All of them will be precious. But some memories, especially those of the really big bulls, will be especially sweet. They will be remembered each fall when you dream again about trophy bulls and should be treated with all the respect due to the magnificent animals that made them possible.

My Best Friend Is a Map

Don't ask my hunting partner about anything. Just ask me and believe that my memory is perfect. I can remember every shot at an elk I ever took. I can recall every step of every trail, how to get to the high benches and elk hideouts, and can remember even the most intimate details of countless drainages. I know I never forget anything about my elk hunting.

But if that's the case, why is it that I find myself forgetting the little things in daily life away from elk country? And, worse yet, why is it that my elk hunting stories differ slightly from those of my partners? The hunting trips were the same. It's just our stories that have changed.

As any honest spouse will testify, our memories aren't quite what they used to be. The longer we rely on them, the worse they get. Or, perhaps, they never were very good to begin with. The details get fuzzy in the passage of time. They get lost in the maze of mountains that we explore. But unfortunately for the elk hunter, these details can mean everything. They can spell the difference between success and failure. Yet too few hunters make a conscious effort to write things down to get the details straight. They rely on their memories instead.

The answer is map work before, during, and after the hunting season. It's one elk hunting exercise, in fact, that can truly take place year-round and can reap as many benefits in January or June as it does during the weeks of actual hunting. In the many maps

Marking elk sightings and kills on a map will eventually lead you to the best areas in all seasons. Bob Zellar photo.

available today, hunters can record their own legacy of elk country. And the information contained on those maps will help you do everything just short of pulling the trigger on an elk.

The importance of maps to an elk hunter goes beyond just the ability to read a map. It also includes purchasing the right kind of maps in the first place and doing the right kinds of things with the ones that you do purchase. The most basic maps for most of us are the forest maps provided by the individual national forests themselves. These maps do a fine job of showing land ownership patterns and the places where private land joins Bureau of Land Management or U.S. Forest Service land. They show roads, some trails, and campgrounds. The same is true of maps provided by the Bureau of Land Management or state fish and game departments. These show land ownership too, and the boundaries of specific hunting areas. But these maps themselves are usually far too broad in scope to do much good in locating a particular hunting spot. They cover too large an area and don't get down to the detail needed to really get to know the country you plan to hunt.

Hunters who really want to learn an area inevitably purchase topographic maps through the U.S. Geological Survey. These topo maps show elevations, water courses, where the draws are, where the timber is located, and the ruggedness of the country, They deal with smaller land area. By looking at the map, you can tell what's over the next ridge without having to climb up and see. They can also tell you how creek drainages come together and where an elk spooked out of one drainage is likely to end up.

Hunters who learn to use a topo map will be able to spot likely elk areas before they ever set foot in them. They can look at the contour lines and pick out the passes where elk move from one drainage to another. They can spot the high benches that could serve as bedding grounds. And they can identify the places that are so rugged that they really don't want to knock an elk down in them, even if they do spot one there.

This kind of study before you get into an area is just one way to use maps, however. The next step is to fight tradition and get them dirty. This goes against the grain of many of us. We see a spotlessly clean and neatly folded map and want to keep it that way. But the best pieces of information you'll have on that map are the ones you end up putting there yourself.

A good example was provided by a couple of hunters from Minnesota who came through Montana a few years back on an elk hunting trip. Before they ever set foot in the mountains, they started asking people what areas were good for hunting. When they got a reply, they'd put a little "x" on the map. Those hunters knew if they asked enough people, got enough straight answers, and put enough of those "x's" on the map, it would give them a much better chance at picking the right hunting spot. The more marks they had on the map, the better they'd know they weren't being misled by a bad answer from a single hunter, too.

Where I have an advantage from living in the area is that I can do this kind of map work on a much more extensive level. And I do.

I have one topo map that has all the places marked where I know people have shot elk during the rifle season. After you've registered thirty, forty, or even fifty kills on the map, it's pretty evident where to hunt. That's better information than a novice or a newcomer can gather in just a season or two. But even if you're able to gather limited information, like the hunters from Minnesota did, it gives you the general idea of a place to start.

Most wild animals are creatures of habit. If something worked for them once, they'll try it again. And they'll usually try it at about the same time of year. As a result, even less-than-complete information can help you eliminate areas that aren't worth trying. If there's a big block of land with only a single "x," it's a sure bet that it won't be as productive as the drainage that is littered with markings. And the more information you can add to it, the better your fine-tuning on your hunting system.

There was a stage in my hunting life when I concentrated hard and heavy on bighorn sheep. I wanted to learn about them in all their separate herds and find success in hunting them when the sheep seasons arrived. I used my kill-locating system on sheep in the Gallatin River drainage, marking each one as to when and where the kill was made. What I found was that there were really only two finger ridges off the main mountains where people consistently took bighorn sheep. With that kind of information in hand, I knew where the migrating bighorns ended up. I also ended up shooting a really big ram because of it.

The better the kill information you can put on your elk map, the better the chance that it will pay off for you in the same way. If you can, find out what drainages, what hillside, what patch of timber, what size elk, and what date a kill was made. Dirty up your map with enough of these things and you should begin to see a correlation of when and where the elk will be at a particular location during the hunting season.

Kill information from the hunting season itself is only one of the things that should appear on your map, however. Your topo map should also be the repository of the knowledge that you gain during the off-season. Researching elk hunting spots in the off-season is actually a never-ending process. The more you learn about an area, the better the chances that the area will pay off when elk season arrives.

One of the most important pieces of information you'll learn is the system of game trails that threads through your chosen piece of hunting country. These game trails will become your highways, just as they're the highways for elk.

Believe me, game trails are the only way to travel in elk country. Animals usually take the easiest route between places. They avoid the deadfall areas. They hit the scattered open parks in the timber that a hunter would otherwise miss. They join feeding areas, bedding areas, mineral licks, summer areas, and wintering grounds. In other words, through the system of game trails, you learn all there is to know about where elk go. But it takes more than just finding the game trails to ensure future success. You have to be able to remember what you've found. That's when the map comes into play again. Dirty your map a little more. Mark in the major game trails and the minor trails that lead to key hunting areas. As you add to the trail system on your map, you'll be surprised how things begin to come together. After mapping several game trails in an area, I noticed how they all seemed to be heading in the same direction. Exploring it a little further, I found they were all headed toward a mineral lick. That, too, was dutifully recorded on the topo map. Other trail systems have led to water holes and wallows. Still others led to hidden parks and meadows where elk headed when they were pushed out of more open feeding areas.

Part of the importance of marking these trail systems on the map is that you won't learn all there is to know in just one season. It takes many years of field work to learn all the little trails. There's one area I've hunted for over fifteen years which has a timbered finger ridge that heads into a big basin. One way to hunt the area is to go up a creek. The distance is three to four miles. The other way is to swing around the head of the basin. That's also three to four miles. But on the topo map is that ridge. If I could only find a trail on that ridge, I'd cut the distance in half.

Logic would tell you that the animals have figured out a way to use that ridge as a shortcut. Logic would also tell you that I could find it. Instead, I can get a trail under it or I can get a trail over it. I've spent ten trips going through deadfall looking for a trail to use that ridge and have yet to find it. Some day, I will. And when I do, it will have a prominent place on my topo map.

This trail will fit in neatly with the other trails that lead me to and from my elk hunting. I've found out the hard way that these trails are always easier and faster to travel on when going from point to point than trying to go cross-country. A direct route might be shorter, but it won't be quicker. Because game trails are always the fastest way from place to place, it always bothers me when I see someone has blazed a new trail. They chop on trees with their axes and leave a permanent mark and feel that they're making the mountains a better place and easier to get around in. Actually, just the opposite is true. If people just learn the game

These Are Elk ■

Map work led us to an area that held many good mule deer, even though hunters working around it never saw them. Don Laubach photo.

trails, they'll get to all the places they need to go.

In addition to trails, there are other features that should be marked on your map as well. It pays to mark some of the feeding areas, bedding areas, and travel routes that elk use when spooked from one area to the next. The map is also there to mark key hunting areas for other species.

Just last fall, I took two of my sons deer hunting to an area that showed up on one of my maps. We walked into the area before daylight and when shooting time arrived, there were deer all around us. My youngest son Ryan got his second deer that day, a decent four-point mule deer. During the course of the day, we looked over twenty-two different mule deer bucks. Yet when we walked out and talked to other hunters, they said they couldn't find a deer that day. I'll be honest with you. I never told those hunters where we went. I figured they could find that out for themselves. Then they could mark it on their own map.

In truth, I'd advise you to do the same. In three or four sentences, you could give away the results of years of scouting in an area. You could also ruin the area for yourself in years to come.

The information that shows up on your topo maps is personal information, whether written out or in code, that will help you get an elk in the future. What you're trying to do is work the odds and increase the chances of getting an elk. Whenever you give away information too freely, you're simply defeating yourself and the time you've put in to gather that information.

On my own map, I have things written out in code. Kills are marked in with an "x," elk sightings with an "s." When things got too complicated with areas for this or that, I went to a colored dot system. I knew what they all meant. But when I wanted to show someone something about the area, I would bring out a different map. I might show people the areas I liked to hunt, but all the details about that area were mine. I didn't give them out. I also tried to be fairly general in my information. If they wanted to learn more, they'd have to do the legwork and enjoy the same sense of discovery that I had whenever I found a new piece of the puzzle.

It seemed to me that it would even be unfair to the elk to let out too much information. Tell too many people about the elk's secrets and you'd change the area for future generations of the animals, too. You'd have given away too much of the secret.

These Are Elk ■

One thing you shouldn't forget is that the information you gather for your map is basically timeless. It took elk decades or even centuries to work out the trail network that leads you to natural features like mineral licks, water holes, and prime feeding areas. Those deep-cut trails through the mountains did not occur overnight. It took thousands and millions of elk hooves pounding them to make them the way they are.

It's also no fluke that a hunter will tell you that he always gets his elk in the same spot every year. He may also tell you that he gets one there at about the same time of the season. Elk are creatures of habit and if you religiously head back to a particular spot that elk use, you'll eventually run into one there.

The facts are that elk are not distributed evenly across a mountain range. There are some spots they like and use a lot. There are others that may rarely, if ever, see an elk. And there are still others that come into play only at certain times of the year or the hunting season. One big key to unraveling the pattern is a good map, a well-used and dirty map covered with information that you gather yourself.

You can learn a lot from maps before you head into the field. But, perhaps, you can learn even more once the hunting has begun. So don't forget your maps when you take to the field. Use them hard in all seasons. They're the best hunting partner you can have and the best friend a hunter ever could want when it comes time to getting an exact picture of what happened long ago.

You see, you and I forget many things. But a good hunting map never forgets.

Picking a Hunting Spot

As an up-and-coming elk hunter, you have pieced together many pieces of the elk hunting puzzle. You know what an elk looks like and some of the places they live. You know about equipment and how it has changed over the years. You know about maps and the importance of extensive scouting to get to know an area. In short, you've learned a good many things in your apprenticeship. But now you have a decision to make. Hunting season has arrived. You've got to decide where you're going to hunt.

If you've done your homework, you've got a good jump on the situation. But there are still some things to be considered before you head into the field.

Probably the three most important factors in picking a hunting spot are your physical capabilities, how much time you have to hunt, and the type of elk you're after. Physical capabilities mean more than just the shape you're in yourself. Even a hunter thick through the middle can go a long way into the backcountry if he happens to be riding a horse. If you're hunting in an area that allows certain forms of motorized vehicles, you might consider using a trail bike, four-wheeler, or snowmobile. Finally, there's people power. You can strap a pack on your back and hike in. Or, if you're imaginative enough like Frank Pickett and his teenage son, Mike, you can turn people power to pedal power. Just last season, the two hunters from Butte, Montana, rode ten-speed and fifteen-speed mountain bikes thirteen miles into the backcountry on old logging roads and downed a five-point bull on opening day of the elk season. It took plenty of work to make those mountain bikes go. In fact, those upslope climbs turned out to be harder than they ever imagined they'd be. But once they got into their chosen hunting area, the only other hunters there had ridden in on horseback. Pedal power had left the foot hunters far behind.

The limiting factor of physical capabilities isn't just getting yourself into the area. It's also what happens when you're successful. How are you going to get yourself and a very limp, very large elk carcass out of there when your hunting is done? You can't just go in blind. You've got to have a plan.

That plan can change with the amount of time you have to hunt. If you're just a weekend warrior, and most elk hunters still are, you've got to be able to get into the area, hunt, and get out again on the same day. That keeps you out of the more remote elk hunting areas. If you have a week or two weeks to hunt, you can go almost anywhere. Then, it doesn't matter if it takes a day or two to reach your hunting area. As long as your back is strong enough, it also doesn't matter if you spend a couple days lugging an elk out to the trailhead on a packframe.

Even if your time is free and easy, getting that animal out remains one of the most important things you have to consider. You've got to consider what happens when you get an elk on the ground. Again, the most important thing is planning. It might be a good friend who lives nearby and owns some horses. It might be a group of hunters who have been together so many years that

If you're looking for a branch-antlered bull, the area in which you're hunting can't be full of only spikes. Frank R. Martin photo

they each have a packframe and even know what part of the elk they're going to carry for the trip back to the trailhead. Or, it might be the Picketts' two mountain bikes, which carried elk parts on two trips over two days to bring that five-point bull back to civilization.

The final consideration in picking a hunting spot is the type of elk you want to take. Do you want a cow or a bull? Is it a big bull or brush bull or spike? That, too, is a major factor in your decision. If you're hunting for a trophy bull, you have to pick a spot where you know trophy bulls exist. And that isn't just anywhere. It may take some extensive research into what Boone and Crockett and state fish and game department records can tell you about where trophy bulls have been taken. Or, if you're hunting with an outfitter, it would be a good idea to find out just how that outfitter defines a trophy bull. It would also pay to find out how many bulls the hunting area might support. If there are only ten bulls total there and only one of the ten qualifies as a trophy in your eyes, then you've got your work cut out for you finding that one single elk.

This kind of research into trophy animals can't be taken lightly. It's going to take more than a casual phone call or a spot check here and there to find a spot with true trophy potential. It reminds me, in fact, of a story told by Terry Koper, outdoor writer for the Milwaukee Sentinel. As part of his research for a hunt in the Rockies, the Wisconsin writer talked to a wildlife biologist in Wyoming who passed on a tale of a man who made just one call to find his hunting area. He called the biologist to ask him exactly where he should go to shoot a mule deer with better than a thirty-inch-wide spread to his antlers. As the biologist told Terry, if he himself knew for sure where there was such a buck, you can bet he'd be out there hunting that muley himself.

Picking the right hunting spot is a matter of matching up physical capabilities, time, and expectations of an elk. Then you begin a process of elimination that will end up with the perfect place to go.

For some hunters, who have scouted just one area, the job isn't difficult. You just go to the place you've scouted. Hunters who know several drainages or mountain ranges have a tougher task. But there are still some key questions. What time of day are you going to hunt? Will you hunt mornings, evenings, or both? Are you hunting the timber during the middle of the day? Will there be other hunters pushing elk toward you? And, once again, how are you going to get the animal out?

That question about getting animals out might seem horribly redundant. Believe me, it's not. I've come across too many elk carcasses in the backcountry where only the heads and backstraps have been removed. Or maybe the head, backstraps, and hind-quarters were gone. The rest of the elk was still lying there and I always wondered whether or not a hunter ever came back to reclaim the rest of the meat. Or, did the hunter realize after getting those pieces out that he just didn't have it in him to pack out the rest. Or, did he have to go back to work the next day and have to leave the elk in the woods until the following weekend and hope to pack out the rest of the meat then. In any of those cases, it's a bad situation. Often, it's illegal. And, equally often, it ends up in the waste of a fine game animal.

There are plenty of stories in elk country about black bears, grizzly bears, mountain lions, coyotes, eagles, magpies, and countless other critters that have eaten, or buried, or ruined an elk carcass that was left in the woods too long.

Another consideration in choosing the right elk hunting spot is how far you can reasonably make it in a day. This is true even

When you pick a hunting spot, you have to know that you can get an animal out. Michael H. Francis photo.

It pays to know everything about your hunting spot before you find yourself in a back-country predicament. Michael H. Francis photo.

if you're hunting out of a backcountry camp. I've bitten off more than I could chew myself several times, picking a hunting spot much further away than I should have. I felt if I only went over the next ridge, that I'd be into elk and away from other hunters. But there are times when that ridge was just too far. You'd get back to camp that night, so physically exhausted that you could barely make it out of the sleeping bag the following morning. If I'd have picked the right hunting spot the first day, I could have hunted two days. Instead, I wore myself down to the point that the second day out was just a token effort.

As you can see, there are a lot of things that go into picking the right elk hunting spot besides the elk themselves. You have to find the spot that suits your methods, your abilities, and the amount of time you have to hunt. You need a working knowledge of that country to know how the elk will use it.

By this point in your elk hunting life, you're ready for the long haul and can make the intelligent decisions that will lead you to elk. You're well along in your apprenticeship as an elk hunter and are ready to start looking for success without having to rely on heavy doses of luck. Now all you need is to fine-tune your knowledge of elk to begin to find success consistently, year after year after year. When you do that, you'll be a full-fledged member of the elk hunting fraternity who makes the most of its elk hunting opportunities and stands a good chance of drawing a bead on a bull anytime they step into the field.

■

ELK COUNTRY

It seems sad to call elk hunting a science. Calling it that gives something that's so much fun a hard and cold definition. But by this time, the elk hunter has begun to learn that a scientific approach to the game will yield far more rewards than a random attack.

The elk are doing certain things at certain times of year. These activities follow a long and rich tradition that has served the animals well over time. It has kept the species fit and helped them survive against the rigors of nature. It has shaped their past and because of that, this tradition will shape their present and future as well.

Our journeyman hunter has come to recognize those patterns and knows that if he's going to fully understand the elk that he seeks, he's going to have to go with them. He'll have to learn their daily lifestyles and tailor his hunting tactics to them. He'll have to learn their seasonal rituals, too, and put himself in the places where elk can be found at particular times of the year.

His storehouse of knowledge is becoming more fine-tuned by this time in his elk hunting career. He knows when, where, and why elk live in certain places. He is beginning to learn how to make the most of this. As a result, his hunting methods and his knowledge of elk are starting to reap rewards.

By this time, the serious elk hunter doesn't realize it, but he has outstripped much of his competition. There are many elk hunters who never make this stage of development. He has left the casual elk hunter behind and has also gone past those who find out that because the sport can be rigorous, they want no more of it.

So it's understandable if the elk hunter takes a moment or two to pat himself on the back. He has come a long way and deserves his moment in the sun. But he knows full well, too, that there is still plenty of trail ahead of him.

Where Elk Wander

Some of the bigger questions facing hunters as they come into their own in the elk hunting game are basic ones that cover elk country and how the animals use it. These questions are logical and necessary.

Before you learn to run in this world, you've got to crawl and walk. And before a hunter can get onto elk on a regular basis, he has to figure out the needs and requirements of the animals themselves and how the elk make the most of the world around them.

First, last, and always, any discussion about elk and the world around them has to cover the things they eat. Elk are a little like the Army. The old saying goes that an Army runs on its stomach. So does an elk. In fact, food is undoubtedly the single most-important driving force in determining where elk will be at any given time of the day, the month, or the year. An elk has to eat. And he'll follow a particular food source anywhere.

That was never more apparent than early this spring when I made the first trip up to my cabin. The cabin sits at about nine-thousand feet elevation, clear at the top of a mountain in the middle of elk country. When I first went up there, there wasn't a bit of animal sign up that high. We had seen the deer and elk further down the slope, feeding on the new green shoots of grass and wildflowers. But none had moved up to cabin level yet. About four weeks later, the green-up reached the nine-thousand-foot level and with it came the wildlife. It was an interesting pattern that showed just how closely the animals were tied to the high nutrition of spring green-up. And it would be a pattern that would be repeated once again before summer was over.

Once the flowers at lower elevations formed their seeds, the deer and elk went down the mountain again. This time, it was to nip off that seed pod, which must have tasted better to them than even the green grass further up the slope. Again, as summer advanced up the mountain, they followed the seed pods up toward the cabin.

This is just one example of how food-specific elk can be. In the book *Elk Talk,* I offered another example of elk keying in on a single food source when I talked about the mushroom mania that grips them in the weeks of late August and September. During that time, there's a particular mushroom with a smooth white cap that emerges in the dark timber in our area. When the mushrooms are out, the elk feed voraciously on them. They wander through the dark timber and actually bite the mushroom off below ground level, then search for the next mushroom. It's far and away the food of choice for them. The elk, in fact, are so intent on finding and eating those mushrooms that a hunter can literally slip up on them unnoticed.

From mushrooms to seed pods to grasses, elk feed on a variety of food sources in their mountain home. It all depends on the time of year as to when, where, and how much they have to eat. While the hunter doesn't have to know each individual plant that make up part of an elk's diet, it's still beneficial to know certain trends and how they come into play. It's my belief, for example, that above everything else, food supply will dictate where you find elk. You've got to have water too, of course. But food is still most important.

In many ways, elk are similar to deer. Both are able to eat a wide variety of grasses and shrubs. But elk are more typically viewed as grazing animals, with mountain grasses as their prime food source. Deer are browsers, with twigs and forbs taking the upper hand in their diet.

The simple facts, however, are that both animals will look for something green first. In spring, that means following the green-up as it moves up the mountain slopes. In fall, it means coming down the mountain to feed on the green areas left in the valleys after grass in the high country has been hit by the first frosts of

The most important ingredient in determining where elk wander is to find the best food supply available at the time. Bob Zellar photo

autumn. In between, they'll choose anything that's high in nutrition to supplement that diet. It might be the flower pods which help to put on weight in a hurry in the months of summer. It could be the mushrooms. Or, when it's available, it might be a nearby alfalfa field, an area of hailed-out wheat or barley, or even a rancher's garden.

In a really dry year, elk might be hard pressed to find food sources. The grass may not be as abundant. It might not have the nutritional value. As a result, the elk will either move to areas with better feed or be forced to stay on their feet longer to find food during the day. During a year of normal or above-average precipitation, that isn't the case. Elk can do their feeding at night and their resting during the day. Cow elk are on the gain through the months of summer and on into September and October. Bulls gain too, until the activity of the rut begins to work away at their fat stores.

Once the snows of winter arrive in earnest, elk are forced to be far less picky in their choice of food. At that time of year, it's

In the old days, elk learned quickly to winter where there were feeding programs to help them along. Doris Whithorn photo.

any grasses within reach that will go to fuel their inner fires. Snow on the ground can help a hunter find their feeding areas. In fact, it's easy to distinguish whether elk are feeding in an area or simply traveling through it. If there are just tracks, it's an area the elk are traveling through. Feeding areas are all pawed up, showing where elk have been digging through the snow to reach the grasses. Feeding areas, whenever possible, are on a steep slope so that when the elk paw the snow away, it tumbles down away from the grass.

If the snow is heavily crusted out in the open or hunting pressure has put the elk in hiding, you can look for elk to feed on the grasses of small open parks scattered through the timber. Or, they could turn to other food sources. There was a time when Montana's fish and game department was looking for stomach samples to determine elk feeding habits and I turned in some from an eight-year-old cow I shot over in the Gallatin drainage. It turned out that this elk had been feeding exclusively on dwarf huckleberry plants. This plant is fairly widespread, but is found only in the timber. Apparently the group of elk the cow came out of had been working over the dwarf huckleberry pretty intensively because her stomach was bloated with the stuff. It also told me that the elk must have been hunted pretty hard because they weren't coming out of the timber at all to look for grasses in the open parks.

The difficulty of finding food in the snow does open up opportunities for the hunter. More calories are being burned by the elk to keep warm in the cold. It takes elk longer to paw up the same amount of grass they could have picked up with ease before the snow arrived. As a result, the elk are up and feeding longer during the months of late fall and winter than they are earlier in the year. They simply have to feed longer to fill up with the same amount of food to meet their previous energy standards.

In a way, after observing elk all my life, it makes me appreciate the biological needs of man. With the amount of food an elk needs to eat, the animal ends up spending hours and hours feeding even in the best of times. In the worst of weather, feeding becomes a full-time job of pawing through deep snow and looking for grasses they hope are plentiful beneath it. Compare that, for a moment, with man who can get by eating three relatively small meals per day and even gain weight on them. It's a lot easier for man to feed when compared to an elk.

As a hunter, we have to take advantage of the difference and key in on the feeding habits of elk. If you find the food source of an elk today, you stand a good chance of finding the elk tomorrow. It's as simple as that.

Elk Sleeping—Do You Disturb?

Elk feed during the night. Elk bed down during the day. Hunters sleep at night. Hunters hunt during the day. It's only natural then that elk hunters would look to the elk bedding areas to shoot an elk. It's the only time they really have to get together. But this kind of logic doesn't take some key factors into account. For one thing, hunting the bedding areas is tough. Making mistakes there is easy. And when you make a mistake in a bedding area, it might mean that you've ended your hunting in that drainage for a good long time.

While elk do spend the bulk of the hunting day in their bedding area, a hunter must make a conscious decision as to whether or not he wants to hunt them there. Whether you hunt them there, in fact, will probably depend on the amount of time you have to

Elk will often bed in thick cover, but will also look for places where they can spot danger before it spots them. Michael H. Francis photo.

hunt. If you're a weekend warrior and don't expect to spend much time in the area, go ahead. You won't be back the next day to bother them. But if you're hunting for a week or so, it might be best to wait until the last few days of your hunt before ignoring the "Elk Asleep—Do Not Disturb" signs and moving in.

There are several reasons for this decision. For one thing, bedding areas are among the most difficult parts of elk country to hunt. They're usually marked by thick stands of jackpines and heavy undergrowth. They're in areas clogged with deadfall or bounded by steep slopes. In short, they're in places where the elk have all the advantage. They can lie quietly and hear anything that comes within earshot. They can see oncoming danger before that danger sees them. And they are bounded by some of the best escape cover that the mountains have to offer. If anything scares them, they can disappear in an instant.

Most elk bedding areas will be on small benches high on north-facing slopes. There are quite a few possible reasons for this. For one thing, the north-facing slopes often have thicker cover than south-facing slopes. It's here you find the deadfall and the thick undergrowth that elk like to hide in. North-facing slopes are also more sheltered from the direct rays of the sun. While the sun bakes the south slopes, the north slopes are cooler. And with the thick coat of fur that elk wear, it's only on cold winter days that they like to bask in the sun.

Because those north-facing slopes have thicker cover, they also attract less human traffic than south slopes. Most hunters go to places where they can see a long way and stay away from areas of thick cover with more limited visibility.

These bedding areas are usually located on benches about two-thirds to three-fourths of the way up the slopes. They choose these level spots not only because they're more comfortable to lie on, but also because they often present a commanding view of the country around them. Elk will often travel several miles to find one of these bedding areas. And once they become traditional bedding areas, they will be used by more than just one bunch of elk. If the conditions are right, they'll be used by any elk that happen to be in the area.

There are some other things about the bedding areas that you should be aware of. A single herd of elk will have more than one bedding area, for example. Also, bedding areas can be changed by the amount of human activity. As hunting season progresses, elk that have been pressed by hunters will head for tougher and tougher country to find security in their bedding areas. The end result can be an area so tough that you wonder how an elk could even move through the deadfall and so cluttered that you wonder how they can find a place big enough to lie down.

Perhaps the most critical thing about deciding to hunt a bedding area, however, is that you risk pushing the elk out of the country if you spook them too badly. If you jump a bunch of elk, take a shot, and get them moving, they're gone. That's the big danger for the hunter who plans to work an area for a long period of time. If he's going to hunt there for a week and spooks all the elk out on the first day, it could be a long, dry week of elk hunting.

Like me, however, most elk hunters are weekend warriors, or at least have the mobility to move from one area to another if all the elk are spooked out. Because I'm limited in the amount of time I can hunt, I like to hunt the bedding areas. If I don't catch the elk out in the open areas or the feeding grounds in the morning, I'll spend the rest of the day in or close to the bedding areas. To me, it's a challenge to walk up on them in their beds. It's also a good place to hit on a track to follow for the rest of the day. So for all the reasons why bedding areas are a logical hunting choice, I like to use them. But I know they aren't easy and I know the deck is stacked against me in terms of surprising a bull there.

The first thing you have to be able to do is recognize a bedding area when you see one. Hunters can run into a lot of beds out in the clearings, but beds there are not of much use to a hunter except to let you know there's elk in the area. Those beds in and near openings are most likely night or evening beds, made while the elk were out in those openings feeding. They might help you figure out an ambush spot for first thing in the morning or last thing at night, but they won't help you during the day. For daytime use, you need to locate bedding areas in the deep dark timber and figure out how to make the most of them.

You have to hunt those bedding areas ever so slowly and carefully. You have to use your binoculars extensively so you can force your eyes to focus on a small area and thoroughly examine it. That way, a hunter can pick out an ear, part of an antler, or see the blink of an eye that can give away an elk's position. Even then, you can easily be startled by elk. When elk are lying down,

If elk aren't pressured, they may bed down out in the open, but most beds in the parks are made during the night. Michael H. Francis photo.

they're hard to see. And many a hunter has found himself sneaking through a bedding area only to find out too late when they explode out of there, that he was literally surrounded by elk that he never saw.

Early in autumn, when the bulls are still with the cows, the cows seem to be more alert than the bulls to danger that's near. At that time, it's the cows that often tip off your presence to the bull and become sort of an early warning system for him. That may be more a matter of the breeding season and how tired the bulls get chasing cows around than anything else, because later in fall, the bulls are just as wary.

The biggest problem that a hunter must overcome in hunting bedding areas is spotting the elk before they spot you. If you can only do that, it opens up numerous possibilities for you. If you don't, your options are limited. The reason is that all elk are not lying side-by-side in a bedding area. They're often scattered in ones and twos over a wide area. If you spot the elk first, even if it's a cow or calf, you have a chance to look over the surrounding area and possibly pick out a bull. If you happen onto a group of bulls and spot one before they spot you, there's the possibility to look that area over for the biggest bull.

There's a certain amount of risk to holding your fire on the first bull you see, of course. I can recall one instance when a hunter and I could have gotten burned that way. We spotted a bull bedded down in the trees. It was a nice six-point. But we decided to stop and look the area over first. We hadn't been glassing long before the six-point started getting nervous. He stood up and was ready to move out when I told the hunter to take him. After we dressed the bull out, I suggested we look the area over. Sure enough, there were several other bulls that had been bedded in the area, but that we never got a chance to see. In the end, the hunter was satisfied with the bull he took, but we never knew about the ones that got away.

This tendency of bulls to bed together during times of the year other than the rut has led to some interesting results when a group of hunters have gotten into a group of elk. One hunter will spot an elk, throw his rifle to his shoulder and shoot, only to find the other bulls were bigger than the one he shot. In the end, his partner or partners who didn't spot the elk end up with bulls that are bigger than his. In hindsight, it's easy to say that the first hunter should have glassed the elk and snuck up on them before he shot. But when you do that, you do run the risk of scaring the bull before you get a chance to shoot. All you can do is size up the situation quickly and hope you make the right decision so you don't lose the bull you have out in front of you.

If you do spook the elk, most times you can kiss them goodbye. They won't be back to use that bedding area for quite some time. The best you can hope for is that they don't leave the country entirely. Perhaps they'll find another bedding area in the same drainage or in the next drainage. But as for that particular spot, they're gone. That's the bad news. But there is some good news, too. The same bedding areas tend to be used by elk year after year after year.

Elk spooked out of one spot today might be back in a week, too. Other elk that come into the area from elsewhere may also move into that spot. I can remember a time when a friend had a cow permit and walked up on a cow and shot her while she still was lying in her bed. We were far enough into the backcountry that we couldn't move her that day, so we went out and got horses and came back the following morning. On the way in, we jumped another cow out of the same area. Whether that cow had been using the bedding area the day before or was new to the area,

I don't know. But normally, once you shoot an elk in a bedding area, it isn't used for a time. It does happen sometimes, however, and that's often enough that if you have a chance to hunt a bedding area again, you should consider doing it.

The important thing to remember is that bedding areas act as attractors for elk. One elk or a group of elk may use a particular bedding area for as long as they're not disturbed there. And even when they move on, the things that attracted those elk there in the first place will make it attractive to other elk that come into the area. So once you find a bedding area, mark its location on your map and tuck the memory away for future reference. It could pay off in the future.

There's one little bench in an area I like to hunt during the rifle season where I've found a lot of beds. I know of three different elk we've taken off that little bench. Sometimes, I've gone through there and not seen an elk or any elk sign. And the next time I went through, the elk were just there.

One of the best ways to find bedding areas is to hunt when there's snow on the ground. At that time of year, tracks from the feeding areas can lead you to the bedding grounds. But the same thing works the other way, too. One of my favorite ways to hunt elk is to follow a fresh set of elk tracks, maybe all day long, until I bumped into the elk that was making them. If you know where the bedding areas are, they're a great place to pick up a fresh set of tracks.

Snow on the ground will also greatly increase your success in hunting the bedding areas. Soft snow will cover your noises as you sneak through the woods. It will also outline the elk better and make them easier to see. But the biggest benefit will come from the way it muffles your footsteps. To hunt a bedding area, you've got to be quiet. You can't have stiff nylon in your clothes or on your backpack that will rub against branches. You can't have ice that freezes on your pants legs and makes them click together when you walk. And you can't move too quickly. The faster you move, the better the chance that you'll make noise and walk past things without seeing them.

Snow can also provide some clues about the elk that use a bedding area. If it's been a while since an elk has used the bed, the snow that its body heat melted will have turned to ice. If the elk used the bed yesterday and it snowed overnight, you can age the bed by the snow. If the bed is obviously fresh, you can read the tracks that lead from it and determine whether you spooked the elk and it's running away or simply walked off. If that elk was just walking, you can follow those tracks and stand a chance of bumping into the animal somewhere along the line.

Another thing to remember is that elk do more than bed down in a bedding area. In fact, one of the best times to hunt a bedding area is when the elk are likely to be on their feet. One of the tricks I like to use is to hunt the slopes where they've been feeding, then wait until late afternoon before I start hunting my way back out. Sometimes, in the afternoon, the elk will get restless, stand up, and start moving around a little bit. It's almost as if they're getting hungry and are anxious to get back to the feeding area. I've also walked through bedding areas and come upon elk that were standing there, motionless, as if waiting to hear a sound that startled them into getting up in the first place. I've literally seen the elk stand there motionless for a half-hour. They never moved. Then, after the half-hour, they've slowly walked off. Or, if their fears prove to be unfounded, they might bed back down again. But having them on their feet made them much easier to spot.

In many ways, hunting bedding areas is a matter of how hard the elk have been pushed. If there are hunters everywhere, the elk will do their best to avoid them. They'll only tolerate being jumped and shot at so many times. The harder they're pushed, the farther they'll go when they're jumped. The harder they're pushed, the more severe the country they'll pick to bed down in. And, the harder they're pushed, the more skittish they'll tend to be in their bedding areas.

You can appreciate the position they're in. They don't like to be scared. They don't like bullets whizzing in their direction. They're trying to hide at a time of day when hunters are about. All they're looking for is a quiet place to sleep away the day.

As a hunter, you have to realize that bedding areas are among the most difficult places to hunt up an elk. On the other hand, they're a place you can find elk even at high noon. They're certainly a place worth exploring as you learn more about elk hunting. Once you learn to take elk from the bedding grounds, you're well on your way to becoming a veteran elk hunter.

Elk on the Go

Elk hunters often find their first success hunting late in the season. When the first blasts of winter storm through the country, elk are forced out of the hiding places where they've been safe and secure during the early and middle parts of the hunting season. Now they're on the move. And with those movements, they put themselves in peril of being spotted by an elk hunter looking to fill his tag.

It should be understood, however, that elk movements aren't limited to the traditional migrations of spring and fall. No, the truth of the matter is that elk are on the move all the time. Movements at other times of the year might be smaller, but these are migrations as well. And even with the big migrations of spring and fall, all elk aren't moving at the same rate. Some movements are fast and long. Others are short.

The thing that elk hunters learn is that with all these movements, the factors behind them are the same. Elk move in search of food, first, foremost, and always. If something eliminates or blocks them from their food source, the elk will move. If better food is available somewhere else, the elk will move. This factor holds true in all seasons. It regulates their movements on the summer range during the warm months of the year and triggers their fall migrations down to the winter range.

A secondary factor in determining their movements is the availability of water. If a water supply dries up during the summer, the elk will move on until they find a new place to drink. If a water supply freezes in winter, elk will do the same. Elk can survive by eating enough snow to quench their thirst, but a supply of open water is by far preferred. Given the choice, they'll seek it out.

Human activity is another key factor in elk movements. If there's a lot of human activity in the area, the elk will move out. That human disturbance factor reminds me of stories I've heard about the old days at Gardiner, which nearly straddles the border between Yellowstone National Park and the state of Montana. In those days, there was a big open flat just over the state line from the park which was closed to hunting. But if you got in the timber above the big flat, that area was open for elk.

The old-timers would wait until all the daybreak hunters had

Elk will follow traditional paths when they head for the winter range during the annual migration. Michael H. Francis photo.

left the timber and then go there themselves, armed with a rubber hose and a big metal pan. They'd beat that pan like a drum and keep up the noise for an hour or more until the elk out on the big flat finally got edgy. When that happened, the elk would head toward what they felt would be the security of the timber. When they got into the timber, they were fair game and the locals would fill their tags. In most instances, daybreak is the best time to hunt elk, but many a local freezer was filled by beating a metal pan drum at noon.

Another factor in elk movements, and one that biologists are just beginning to uncover the fine details about, is tradition. It wasn't that hunters and biologists didn't know that tradition played a role in elk movements. It was just that they didn't realize how well-defined the traditions of mountain wildlife could be and how complicated and exacting it was.

There's no tradition that seems to be as well-defined as the move to the winter range with the coming of winter. Each year, elk respond to stimulus in the world around them and make the move. It's that movement that has led many hunters to their first elk and some hunters to their annual elk.

But to understand it, you have to look at elk in their basic year-round living groups and forget about the giant herds on the winter range. Each of these basic groups have individual traditions passed down through generations of elk. And those traditions have stood the test of time.

Some elk, for example, may leave their summer ranges and begin their fall migrations with the first skiff of snow in September and travel for forty miles or more to reach a particular winter range. They may, in fact, pass up other winter ranges along the way to get to the exact spot where their ancestors wintered. The reason they do this is that other elk, which may have waited longer to move or may have chosen those other winter ranges, died because of it. If they waited too long, winter snows might have blocked their way. If they chose the other winter ranges, they may not have been as reliable during the really tough years. As a result, the natural selection process chose that group of elk to make that movement at that exact time in order to survive.

These movements can be remarkably quick. There was one collared cow elk that was shot near Gardiner, for example, which was located the day before about forty miles away. That cow had made the forty-mile move in just twenty-four hours. While most elk won't travel that far, there are enough far-flung herd segments feeding a good winter range that it really isn't that much out of the ordinary.

Just as the long-traveling early migrators must leave with the first snowflakes to make it over mountain passes to reach the winter range, there are other elk which wait until the last minute and make short migrations. These elk often live their entire lives in the same drainage, moving up to the head of it in spring and summer and then coming back down in late fall to the wintering grounds.

These migrations move in stages, with various herd segments taking off at different times. In the migrations we have in this area, it's often the middle-aged bulls that will move first. These bulls will take a higher migration track than the cows that will come next. They will stay in the timber instead of coming through the openings. And they may stop short of what people view as the traditional wintering range, choosing instead to remain a bit higher in elevation for the winter.

The next herd segment out is the big bunches of cows and calves, which may also have a few young bulls with them. These are the big migrations where long lines of elk can string out for a mile or more as they move through elk country.

Finally, the last herd segment that moves is the big bulls. Like the other bulls that moved earlier, this group too will usually stick to the timber and spend their winters in the relative isolation of areas a bit higher than the traditional winter range. It's tough country up there, but the bulls have done it that way for centuries.

Exactly how tough that winter can be was shown to me a number of years ago when I went cross-country skiing in the mountains near my home. I got into an area where the snow was seven to eight feet deep, yet the bulls were spending the winter on that mountain slope, pawing their way down and making huge holes as they dug their way down to the grass. When I skied toward the group of bulls there, one winter-weary bull tried to run up the hill and ended up falling over backwards on his antlers. It was a position he couldn't get up from in his weakened condition. So I shook my head for the poor creature and skied away.

After spending the night in the high country, I skied out the next day, going past the same spot. Surprisingly, the bull had gotten himself out of the predicament of the day before. But, once again, he tried to run up the slope and fell backwards on his antlers the same way. I felt like kicking myself as I skied out of there, but I really figured the elk had died the night before. As it was, when I returned that spring, I found where the bull had winter-killed and where the predators had worked him over. It turned out that the deep hole he had dug for himself in order to get food, had turned out to be his grave.

I can't help but think of that bull when I think about the traditions that go into elk migrations. Right then and there, the seeds of a tradition died. It wasn't meant to be that elk should choose to winter on that slope, where eight feet of snow could trap them in a hole. Other elk that moved to more suitable winter quarters survived the snows that year. Their traditions were passed on and will be repeated for generations of elk to come.

Many times, the key ingredient in keeping the migratory traditions alive is the lead cow. This is the wise old girl that has made the journey many times before. She learned the time to leave, the way to go, and where to spend the winter from other lead cows in earlier years.

Some believe, in fact, that if you shoot the first bunch of

During the late season, hunters should be prepared to walk in deep snow as they look for elk. Michael H. Francis photo.

migrating elk or shoot the lead cows, that you can actually kill the migratory tradition of a herd of elk. If those old cows die, they won't have a chance to train the younger animals where to go. There is some evidence to support this. When a lead cow is shot and killed, the rest of the herd will often just mill around, not knowing where to go. Given enough hunters with enough permits, the entire herd could be shot before they'd get a notion how to escape. Because of that, hunters will often stay away from the lead cow, if they have a choice. That way, they know the elk will return to that spot next year.

One final thing that a hunter learns early in his elk hunting life is that the bulk of the migratory movements of elk take place at night. Perhaps that's because they have to cross so much open ground in their migrations. Perhaps, it's because the nights are cooler and might make for easier traveling. But whatever the reason, elk often begin their migrations just before dark and will walk all night long.

For the elk hunter, that means dawn could find some new elk in the country. It could mean that country which was barren of tracks the day before suddenly is littered with the signs of elk on the move. And it could mean that even after several fruitless days of looking for elk, that this day could be full of them.

An old outfitter friend of mine, Wayne Hoppe, told me about just such a day which showed how migration routes and traditions can combine with new elk to make for some strange sights. In the old days, he said, hunter's cars would line up bumper to bumper on the road between Gardiner and Jardine which crossed one of the major migration routes in the area. The elk would migrate from south to north during the night and the hunters would head north the following morning to go after them. It didn't take much shooting at first light for the elk to realize they had moved into a dangerous area. So, often they'd head back, trying to retrace their tracks and head into the closed area south of the road. Hoppe said there were times when the elk would come to that string of cars and literally leap over them in a single bound in their search for safety.

Hunters also learn early in their careers that going after elk on the migration route is probably some of the easiest hunting available as far as success goes. Those migrating elk have one thought in mind and that's to get to an area with some food. In

If elk don't choose the right spot to spend the winter, they very likely will starve before spring arrives. Michael H. Francis photo.

that quest, they often let their safeguards down. They're not as quick to react as they are during the earlier parts of the season when they're fat and happy and in the security of their summer and fall ranges.

By the time the big migration arrives, the elk know they're in for some weather and they know the hardships of winter will soon be upon them. They've started to use their stores of summer fat and they're losing weight. They're losing their ability to be as strong as they were at the start of the season. And they're not as sharp as they were when getting a full belly was less of a full-time job.

Those conditions give elk hunters a bit of an advantage over the elk they seek. It's just enough of an advantage that many a hunter has scored on his first bull during the fall migration. Some hunters wait for the migration every year before picking up their elk rifles and heading out for the hunt. Once you learn the migratory tradition of elk on the go, you stand a good chance of cashing in on that knowledge every year.

Watching the Weather

Many's the time that I've thanked my lucky stars that I live in

If you play the weather right, you could end up with a big bull to skid back toward your vehicle. Mark Henckel photo.

the heart of elk country. Frankly, it gives me an advantage in so many ways over so many others who seek the monarchs of the mountains.

We've talked about how it can help a hunter in his scouting by being able to walk through his hunting country at other times of the year. We've talked about how it gives a hunter access to others who have found success and are available to answer your questions. But what we haven't talked about is how something as simple as being able to watch the weather can help a hunter to find consistent success in the elk woods.

Along with food, water, and tradition, weather also plays a key role in elk movements. By watching the weather, you can have a pretty good idea of when elk are going to move, where they're going to hide, and when and where they're going to feed.

This is the type of information that a hunter picks up along the way rather early in his hunting career. But it's also information that can be added to and refined as he continues his hunting life.

The most obvious and dynamic weather factor that works on elk is a weather front late in the season. By then, winter is often well on its way. The early-migrating elk have left their summer ranges, but the big push hasn't arrived yet. If a hunter knows one of these storm fronts is on its way, he'll notice that elk are moving ahead of the front. Elk will be feeding more actively. They will be moving on their migration routes. And the hunter who can take advantage of the situation the day before the front arrives can often get his bull and get out before the storm hits.

I can recall a day when I was out filming with wildlife cinematographer Gordon Eastman when we came across a string of elk moving along in single file that stretched out for a mile. This movement came just before dark on that migration trail. It heralded a change in the weather. The following day, a big front came through and dumped heavy snow.

During the storm itself, elk rarely move. Often showing more sense than the hunters who seek them, they'll hole up during the brunt of the storm and let it blow over. They'll head for their hideaways in the timber and stay out of the open places where the storm rages.

Finally, when the storm subsides, the elk will move again. This movement, on the day after the storm, can be the most dramatic of them all. If the storm was a big one, elk may be moving all over the place. Cows and calves will string out through the open parks and meadows. Bulls will travel higher up the slope through the timber. At times, when you look at the tracks they leave behind, it seems as if all elk everywhere are on the move for new and better pastures.

In fact, I know of hunters who have one single hunting strategy toward the end of the hunting season. They watch the weather and hole up during the storms. On the day after the storm, they drive to their hunting area knowing the elk will be moving into it. Then, on the second morning after the storm, they hunt. By that time, the new elk have had a chance to move into the country and the hunters are there and ready for them.

These before-storm and after-storm movements can be sizable. Elk can and will move a long way. In fact, the hunter who hits the tracks of a migrating elk may find there's just no way to catch up to them.

An example of how extensive those movements could be was shown to me a number of years ago when I rode into elk country to set up camp with a cousin and several other friends. We were riding toward a spot eight miles past the end of the road and had traveled about five miles when we spotted two nice bulls feeding on a mountain slope about a mile in the distance. It was one of those times when you really didn't know what to do.

We could have gone after the bulls then. But if we did, we would have doomed ourselves to setting up camp in the dark. With ten horses to care for, a full camp to set up, and the sky looking like there might be some bad weather afoot, we decided to wait until the following morning to go after the bulls. We could ride the three miles back in the darkness, get above the bulls, and be there at first light to fill a couple of tags.

As if to rub it in, while we were setting up camp, we spotted a group of cows feeding in a clearing across the canyon from our camp. Those were fair game too, under the hunting regulations of the time, and one of our group really wanted to hang his tag on a cow that year.

The following morning, we headed after the bulls but found only their tracks heading down a slope so steep we couldn't follow them. The bulls had pulled out during the night. With no way to follow the bulls' tracks, we turned our attention to the cows, hoping to circle high and move in from above them. The hunting pattern for the rest of the day was set while making that big circle when we cut the two bulls' tracks heading up the canyon. Two in the group decided to follow them. Others decided to stick with the cows. It was a member of the latter group that made meat that day. He jumped a cow from her bed in the timber above the clearing and made a good shot. As for the two hunters who decided to go after the bulls, they followed those tracks for fifteen miles without ever jumping the elk, seeing them, or having a chance to take a shot.

Those bulls might have moved because of the weather front that did dump snow that second night out. It's possible that something else might have sparked their migration. In either event, they moved more than fifteen miles and through at least two creek drainages without stopping. To my way of thinking, it's the weather that made them move. They were moving ahead of the storm.

Another big influence on elk and where you find them is the wind. Of all the weather factors, this one is perhaps the most underrated. Unlike snow and cold weather, wind is more of a hidden influence. Yet it determines where elk are going to bed down and when and where they'll be feeding.

Like humans, elk don't like wind. It confuses their senses of hearing and smell. In cold weather, it saps their energy and they burn up too many calories trying to keep warm. Wind also changes the world around them, drifting grass-rich draws full of snow and blowing ridge-tops clear.

The old rule of thumb was that if the wind was blowing thirty miles per hour, the elk would move into the timber. My own findings are that it doesn't take a wind nearly that strong to move elk into different areas. If the wind blows hard, you won't have any elk out in the open. If the wind blows hard for several days, you may find that elk will spend all that time in the timber, feeding there and bedding there. Then, when the wind stops, all the elk will move back out and feed in the open areas. Not only will they be feeding there at normal times, but you may find that they're out in the open much longer to make up for the nutritional value they lost by staying in the timber during the period of strong winds.

Elk will do what they have to do to reduce the effects of heat loss. The protection of the trees will shelter them from the wind. They can rest there without burning up so many calories to keep themselves warm. There's some food available, even if it isn't of the same high quality as out in the open. It's the perfect place to spend the windiest days.

On days when the wind isn't blowing as strong, you still might find the elk using sheltered hillsides. If they can find an open slope that's out of the wind, they'll feed there. Under those conditions, they still get the high nutritional value without losing body heat. They can also better use their senses of smell and hearing to detect the presence of danger.

The reaction of elk to the wind can also help you plan strategy in certain hunting situations. If you're glassing a distant slope and spot a bunch of bedded elk, pay special attention to the direction they're facing. Elk tend to stand and bed with their noses into the wind. All you have to do is figure out which way most of the noses are pointing and you know the wind direction and how to plan your stalk.

Finally, there's just plain cold weather that affects where and when you'll see elk. Elk battle cold from the mid-point of most elk seasons clear until spring. It's the big killer of the young and the old and elk must learn to cope with it if they hope to survive to see spring. In fact, cold plays against all other weather factors to create conditions where lost body heat will mean burning up critical stores of fat.

A hunter should understand, however, that elk are well suited to the cold. They can take conditions much tougher than the people who hunt for them. One time, I was hunting with outdoor writer Jim Zumbo and my son, Kirk, during winter conditions toward the tail end of the season. That morning, Kirk shot his first bull elk, a good five-point. But the thing that sticks in my mind is that sometime during the bitter cold night before, that bull had swum the river. I know, because even though it was four miles from the river where Kirk shot him, the bull was still coated with ice. They must be unbelievably tough to stand that kind of cold. Yet it's just part of their life-long routine and they grow used to it.

Changes from warm weather to cold weather also determine elk movements. If there's snow on the ground, warm weather will melt it while a return to cold conditions will form a thick crust. Crusted snow is something elk don't like for several reasons. Some say they don't like to walk in it because there's a tender spot on their hooves that hurts them as they walk through the crust. As a result, crusted snow can start elk migrations even when the snow isn't very deep and can speed them up as elk travel in search of uncrusted areas. The crust also makes it more difficult for elk to paw down through the snow to get to the grass below when they're feeding.

When hunting in crusted conditions, a hunter should be especially alert in late afternoon because the warmth of the day will sometimes soften the crust or melt it off completely. Elk, knowing that, will move out in the open to feed during the late afternoon to take advantage of the softer snow.

Changes in weather will also affect the migrations of elk. They may move toward the winter range in periods of snow and cold, then stop when the weather eases up. If the weather moderates and the food is good, they may stay there for a time, turning their stopping point into something of a staging area until the next shot of snow and cold comes through. If the weather really warms up and the snow melts off, the elk might even pull back into higher elevations in something of a mid-migration retreat. These movements will all depend on the availability of food and the amount of people pressure that pushes the elk around.

The coming of a storm front will affect the way the elk move both before the storm and after it. Michael H. Francis photo.

Two days after the storm could be the perfect time to find out that elk have moved into your hunting area. Michael H. Francis photo.

Almost inevitably, however, the conditions of winter will eventually force elk onto the winter ranges. Cold, wind, and snow will put elk into a deficit situation in terms of their reserves of stored fat. They'll have to feed longer to take in as much food as they can. In all but the windy times, they'll have to move out into the open to find the best food. In short, they'll have to expose themselves to hunters.

Hunters who watch the weather and know how elk will react to it, will put themselves in a position where a late-season bull or cow is well within their reach.

■

PLAIN OLD HUNTING

Make way for the veteran elk hunter and bow when he passes. Here is a hunter who knows where to go and what to do when he gets there.

By this time, an elk hunter has paid his dues both to elk country and the elk that inhabit it. He can map out a plan of attack that will take him to elk at any time of the season. He knows where the elk are and what they'll be doing when he gets there.

If there is such a thing as a most fulfilling stage of development in an elk hunter, this is surely it. His base of knowledge provides him with all the things he needs to know. He knows the country. He knows the elk. He knows the tactics.

If he wants to go after an early-morning elk, he knows how to find out what open parks and meadows they will be using. Just stand back and give him the time to scope out the situation the evening before and be ready to load your rifles in dawn's first light.

When the elk think they're tucked away safely within the black timber, the elk hunter comes equipped to ferret them out of there, too. Just give him a patch of black timber during the middle of the day where others fear to tread and stand back. It's a home away from home for him.

Perhaps even more important, during those mid-season doldrums when no one else is getting elk, the elk hunter knows about the hidey holes where the elk go in the toughest of times. If it's possible to get in there, and get the elk out when you get him, the elk hunter can find them and fill his tag.

By this time, luck is working on his side. The elk hunter knows that while the novice may get lucky some of the time, the odds are with him that he'll make his own luck when he needs it. When it comes down to just plain elk hunting, this hunter knows the tactics to get the job done.

Stalking the Black Timber

In a way, the black timber of elk country would make the perfect setting for a remake of one of those old African adventure movies. All it would take is just a few minor script changes.

You could still have the Great White Hunter. You could have the Number One Gun Bearer acting as a guide. And you could have all the mystery of the search for something as grand as the mythical elephant graveyard with its cache of precious ivory.

I close my eyes and can see it all now.

"Yes, Bwana, there is such a place filled with ivory-tipped elk antlers. It's the place where all the big bulls go," the gun bearer would say.

"Could there be such a place? How can I get there before the other hunters find it and rob it of its six-points?" the Great White Hunter would answer.

"The path is a dangerous one. It is filled with great confusion and peril," the gun bearer would say. "It cuts deep into the darkest black timber where others fear to go. The trees close in on you. The ground beneath your feet disappears in a tangle of tree trunks and branches. The sky is blotted out by limbs above. And you fear you never will come back alive."

"Well, Gun Bearer, if that's the case, forget it. I might muss my crisply starched woolens. Let's go look for elk on this open ridge instead...."

So much for great adventure. So much for getting an elk in the middle of the day in the middle of the season, too. Yet that's the attitude that most hunters take when they bump into one of those patches of black timber.

The black timber of elk country is really the jungle of the North. It's as thick and impenetrable as any in a tropical climate, though it differs from them in that there are other places to go where hunters can avoid it. And most hunters do. They skirt the edges, look into parks and meadows, climb the open ridges, and venture into the heavy deadfall only as a last resort.

First of all, it should be pointed out that black timber isn't really black timber at all. It's just that the trees are thicker there and usually tall. The trees block out the sunshine and leave the dark timber in a state of near-constant shade. These areas are usually found on north-facing slopes and, because they avoid the direct rays of the sun, often are moister and cooler than slopes that catch more of the sun. With its thicker stands of trees and years of snow, wind, rain, and wood-eating insects, you also end up with a considerable amount of deadfall on these slopes. It's that deadfall, in fact, that makes them so seemingly impenetrable.

But black timber is the home of the elk. Most of their daylight hours are spent there. It's their inner sanctum, the place they go when all else fails them. In short, when they want to get away from hunters, the black timber is the place they go.

Yet black timber is far from a favorite spot for hunters. Perhaps it's because we have long-reaching guns now that are able to place a bullet with pinpoint accuracy at several hundred yards. Maybe it's something deep in our psyche from eons past that tells us to stay out of close places where we become vulnerable to predators. Or, it could simply be the fact that it's damn tough stuff to get through. Whatever the reason, if you want solitude in even the most congested hunting situations, stay away from the parks and meadows and head for the black timber.

For my part, I love the stuff. It's one place where I know there always will be elk. It's also a spot where you have to face elk on their own terms, using all your senses to detect them before they use all their senses to detect you.

That doesn't mean that just because you're hunting in black timber you're guaranteed an elk. In that way, it's just like the open hillsides. There are some good spots and some bad spots. And, unfortunately, most of the good spots will be found in on-the-ground, tough-it-out, buck-the-brush fashion.

What I've found is that the best spots in the timber are the little areas where you have springs emerging from the ground. You

Plain Old Elk Hunting

If an elk stands up, it gives you a much better opportunity to spot him in the dark timber. Michael H. Francis photo.

Using binoculars to force yourself to look at a small area will help you spot the pieces of elk that add up to a nice bull. Michael H. Francis photo.

Plain Old Elk Hunting ■

might have a hidden draw there with some grassy slopes. And, best of all, you might have a little bench or a series of little benches about two-thirds of the way up the slope. Given the choice, I'd hunt my way down through the series of benches. That way, I'd be above the elk and have a better chance of spotting them. But if I were at the bottom of the slope and had to work my way up, I'd do it in long, angled sweeps across the mountainside. It seems you never have much luck going straight up the slope.

When you find the benches, you'll notice that the elk will have several escape routes. That's what makes them excellent places for elk to bed down. They may not be permanent bedding areas for elk, but they are places that elk will stay for a short period of time, especially when pushed during the hunting season.

The biggest problem that hunters face is that they have to hunt these areas very quietly. The elk are usually bedded down or are standing still, which gives the animals the advantage of being able to use their hearing. Complicating things is the tangle of fallen logs and branches on the ground. Sometimes, you may find yourself walking on the trunks of fallen trees for several hundred feet without ever touching the ground. To be able to do this, and do it quietly, and still concentrate on your hunting is a skill that wasn't born in everyone. Sometimes, you're three or four feet up in the air on the latticework of downed timber. Other times, you may have to backtrack or go far to the side to get around an obstacle.

The first thing you find out about these deadfall jungles is that there often aren't any trails through them. Instead of following a trail, the elk just fan out and pick their way through. That doesn't mean, however, that the deadfall poses much of a problem for elk. Somehow, some way, elk can cruise through these areas with ease. They do it with about as much difficulty as a hunter can walk a clean trail. Don't ask me how. They just do.

Hunting the black timber is usually best during the mid-day hours. With tracking snow, it's even better. But you have to be able to hunt slowly and quietly to get game. Because some hunters simply can't hunt quietly, they often sit or stand in the dark timber instead. Even though there often aren't any trails to watch, a hunter with a keen eye should be able to spot elk sign in other ways. Often, there are elk droppings, rubs, or tracks that give the elk's presence away. By looking for them, you can find the general areas where elk tend to move through. If there's a plus to this kind of hunting, it's that a hunter can use his own senses to their fullest in his quest for an elk. You can hear the sound of the footfalls of an elk. You can smell their presence when they get near. And you can watch for the slightest movements that will give them away.

For my own part, however, I'd rather stalk elk in the black timber. It's a challenge to walk up on an elk in his own environment. But no matter how good you get, you'll never do it every time. The odds are stacked too heavily against you. But even if you do it once, you'll get a thrill from working an elk on his own turf.

One thing to remember when you're hunting the dark timber is that you have to be able to get an elk out of there, too, after you knock them down. That's not as simple as it sounds. I can remember one occasion when a friend knocked down a bull and it took us an entire day just to cut a trail for the horses in to the spot where the elk was down. Never forget the old truism about elk that there are some places where you had better pack a lighter and a loaf of bread and eat the elk on the spot, because you'll never get them out of there.

A hunter should remember that there are many more things that live in the black timber besides elk. In fact, I've always found that you stand a better chance of finding elk if you're looking in areas that have other animals. If you see squirrels and birds, that's a good sign. If you find small animals, you often find the big ones, too. And even if you don't find elk, you're likely to see some things you've never seen before.

One time a few years back, I was hunting with my son Wade through a patch of deadfall timber when I walked up on a pine marten that had just caught a squirrel. That's a sight that most hunters have never seen, but it's one that deadfall hunters do chance upon from time to time. When the marten spotted me, he took off with the squirrel in his mouth and I ran after him until he raced up a log that was leaning against a tree. The marten finally stopped when he was head high with me. And he began to eat the squirrel. It was quite a sight. That marten ate everything— the fur, the head, the paws. By the time Wade came over, only the tail of the squirrel was left and he started on that about the way a human eats a carrot. When he got down to the very end, where there wasn't anything left but hair, the marten spit it out, lifted his rear leg as if in a final salute, and came down the log. He ran over to a live tree, went up it to a head-high branch with a bough on it, curled his tail over his head, and went to sleep. Naturally, we had no camera with us. So that's right where we left him as we went on in search of elk.

Hunters in the black timber have to be prepared to see elk at any time. But they also have to be ready to make decisions if the elk see them first. Often, the first hint a hunter has that there are elk in the area is when you hear them moving off out in front of you or smell them. When that happens, a hunter basically has two choices. He can go after them slowly. Or, he can go after them fast.

The slow method works best if the elk also is moving out slowly. Perhaps they haven't seen you, but were simply spooked by the presence of something else in their area. Sometimes, these animals just walk away. If they're not sure what spooked them, the hunter can use a cow call and give the elk the impression that it's just another elk that's wandered into the area. The elk will often stop, stand, and look back in the direction from which the cow call came. That can give the hunter a second chance to sneak up on the animal that could result in a shot at the elk.

One hunting friend of mine took the tactic one step further. When he jumped an elk, he would stop competely for a full half-hour, then try and circle high above the elk and drop down about where he figured the elk would have stopped his escape. He found that the elk often went through a clearing and then stopped just inside the timber on the opposite side. His tactic would often bring him in contact with the animal an hour or more after he jumped it. Yet he often found the animal still standing after all that time, intently watching his back trail.

The fast method of following up a jumped elk is to simply run as fast as you can in the direction where the elk went. This may sound like a futile gesture in the face of how fast an elk can move through the mountains, but it's a plan of attack that works far better than you'd ever believe. Many times, you'll run into more than just the elk you jumped, because other animals will be bedded in the same general area. Other times, your hurry-up flight will surprise the animals so much that they'll stop and turn to see what's chasing them.

The black timber is the best place of all to look for a bull during the middle of the day. Michael H. Francis photo.

That very thing happened once when I was hunting with Bob McBride. We jumped some elk at the edge of some little jackpines. We smelled them first, and then we heard them. The timber itself was heavy, but they ran downhill, and there was only a couple of inches of snow on the ground. Bob and I took off after them. Bob saw the tracks of the main bunch and went that way. I spotted where a couple of elk had peeled off of the main bunch so I went that way. It wasn't over a hundred yards of downhill running before the elk started to sidehill the slope. And, when they heard me coming, they stopped to look. By that time, I was on them and got a shot before they had a chance to bolt away again. The fast followup had helped me to a nice six-point bull.

For the most part, a hunter has to play it by ear as to which method he's going to use when he jumps elk. It's a fact of life that some of the time, the hunter is going to make the wrong choice.

The key to successful hunting in the black timber is to locate the parts of it that the elk like to stay in. In some areas, they simply pass through. But in others, they're likely to hold there for several hours or even several weeks during the course of the hunting season.

The best spots, of course, have all the ingredients of life that an elk needs. They have water, food, and secure bedding areas. In places like this, it's not uncommon for a good bull to hole up for the entire hunting season, safe from hunters until the cold and snow of winter forces him to pull out for the migration to the winter range. When a hunter finds a place like this, it's like a jewel gleaming through the deadfall. And, like a jewel, it should be treated with reverence and respect, and should be dutifully marked on the hunting map.

Over the years, these spots are as important to an elk as a prime feeding area, a mineral lick, or a breeding-time wallow. They have all the ingredients to attract elk year after year after year. And the hunter who learns where they are and how to work them stands a chance of pulling an elk out of them on a regular basis.

One word of warning should also be attached to any discussion of hunting elk in the timber. That warning is that hunters stand a good chance of getting confused. When your entire world is made up of tangles of logs beneath you and bushy trees all around, it's easy to get turned around. Before you step into the deadfall jungle, a hunter should look around at the surrounding mountains and get some points of reference that will help him when he comes back out. If the sun is available, it's also good to note its location in regard to where the hunter expects to emerge. But this is one time when a hunter should also make use of his compass almost every step of the way. By taking compass readings, a hunter can better pick his destination no matter how many times the black timber and deadfall might turn him around.

Over time, a hunter should also make use of landmarks within the black timber areas, both to help find his way through them and to stand a better chance of comparing notes with his partners when the hunting is done. If you can talk about places like the big rock, the blowdown, the twisted tree, or anything else that helps to pinpoint a location, you can tap your partner's knowledge as well as your own about a particular patch of black timber that might help you both to an elk in the future.

Perhaps the most important thing that elk hunters should learn about the black timber is that it should be included in their hunting plans. It holds elk when other places do not. And, it holds them during the time of day when a hunter has a chance to get after them. That may go against the grain of most elk hunters who'd rather be out in the open where they can see a long way. But it's a tactic that works well for the patient hunter who can move through the timber slowly and quietly.

That's why when others choose parks and meadows to hunt, I'll take the challenge of the deadfall and the elk that live within it. Give me black timber for elk hunting anytime.

Hunting the Parks and Meadows

Elk eat grass. Open parks and meadows are full of grass. Therefore, logic would tell you that the place to hunt elk is in the parks and meadows. After all, an elk has to eat.

The trouble with this theory is that it's too simplistic to take into account all the variables involved in elk hunting. In fact, this beginners' notion doesn't take into account even the most basic of problems facing an elk hunter.

By the time a hunter has been at the game for a number of years, by which time he learns that open parks and meadows are basically the same thing but are named differently in different parts of elk country, he also learns that these clearings are beautiful to look at, but don't hold elk very often during daylight hours. The secret of success in making the most of open parks and meadows is that you have to do your scouting first. You have to get some unwitting cooperation from other hunters. And, you have to get up pretty darn early in the morning or be willing to make it back to camp long past sundown. Then, and only then, will open parks pay off for you.

Elk use these clearings for one thing only—as a food source. Elk are in them when they're feeding. And for feeding, they're in them during late evening, throughout the night, and early in the morning. As a result, a hunter must be at the right open park at first light or in the first half-hour of shooting time. Or, he must be there during the last minutes of the shooting day. Being there at any other time, for the most part, is a waste of precious elk hunting season.

But even then, you can't just go out and blunder your way through the high country meadows and expect to get an elk, even if you're there at the right times of day. Hunting blind will lead to more of a waste of the season.

Let me give you an example. In the mountains where I hunt, there are many open parks. One of them is a beauty that I've been watching for the past fifteen years. That mountain meadow seems to have everything. In the summer, the grass grows tall and thick and the ground is lush with wildflowers. To see the abundant food source, you'd think elk and deer would be there all the time. But during spring, summer, and most of fall, very few animals use the grass in that park. The only time I've ever observed animals in the opening is during late fall. Generally, it's about two weeks after the first heavy snow hits. Then, animals move onto that range and start feeding on it. From that starting point, it's a great hunting spot for about two weeks. Then, the animals move off it again. Why that beautiful open park is used by elk just during that short span is a mystery to me. But there's some limiting factor there for the elk. And there's an equally limiting factor working on the hunters who choose to go there during any other time of the season. Those hunters have blindly picked the wrong place to look for elk and are wasting their time.

A far better plan of attack is to put your scouting talents to good use before you pick your park. In fact, it's the only way to hunt them. And, more elk have been killed this way than in any other single method I know.

All it involves is using your binoculars or spotting scope to locate elk in the open parks the evening before you plan to hunt. A hunter should pick a good observation point and plan to sit there until dark, glassing all the open parks within sight to see which ones the elk are using. Once you spot the elk, you can figure out the strategies it will take to get to them before daylight the following morning. If things go according to plan, the elk will probably still be there at first light.

A hunter has to get there bright and early, however. The heavier the hunting pressure, the quicker those elk will be moving out of the open parks and back to the safety of black timber to spend the day. Another factor at work with heavy hunting pressure is the likelihood that some other hunters will be using the same scouting strategy and be working the same bunch of elk the following morning.

There's really no way of knowing how many hunters might be working those elk. But if there are enough hunters in your group, you might work out an alternate strategy the way we learned to over the years. If we thought there might be other hunters, we tried to figure out where the elk would go once they were spooked out of the opening. Then we'd send part of our group to cover the escape route and head them off. It was a tactic that didn't work everytime, but it worked often enough that it did pay off over the years.

To do that, you had to know the country you were hunting. You also had to know the types of areas that elk would use when they were or were not being pressured by hunters. One rule of thumb that an experienced hunter knows is that elk will start using smaller and more remote clearings as they feel the pressure of hunters. In the opening days of the season, for example, the elk might be found in the big parks in areas that are readily accessible. But as they get pushed out of them, they'll pull back into places where it's tougher for the hunters to find them.

An elk hunter who plans to hunt the open parks will have to take this into account. It may be, for example, that a hunter needs to hike in a mile or more and may have to get into one specific vantage point that will give him a view of a remote opening. Instead of the classic big parks, the elk may use smaller openings that are tucked into places where hunters rarely go. And a hunter

An open slope can provide you with an early morning elk if you do your scouting before you head there. John Potter photo.

might find that elk show up only during the last minutes of light when a good pair of binoculars needs all the light-gathering properties it can muster to spot them.

There was one season when my brother Doug and I spotted three bulls that were putting all of these tactics to use. These elk were using a park just one hundred yards wide and three hundred yards long that was located high on the mountain about three thousand feet above the nearest road. For two days, we watched them emerge from the timber in the last minutes of daylight and feed in that little park. On the third evening, we went after them.

As we eased into position, we could see the tracks that the bulls had been leaving in the snow each evening. Before morning's light, they headed back toward a heavily-timbered bench where they would hide all day. We just sat there and waited. And just before dark, the three bulls emerged, giving Doug a hundred-yard shot and a good six-point bull. If the hunt was easy, it was because we had done our homework and knew exactly what the elk would do.

A fine point of our success on that trip was knowing how long it would take us to get to the area and arriving there on time. I know, because a similar plan went awry for just that reason.

This time, it was a group of elk spotted one evening clear back at the head of a high mountain basin. Through binoculars, we could see the area had scattered timber and a few open parks. Looking at our topo maps, we could see how far it was to get there. So we figured out our walking time, allowing three hours of hiking in darkness to get us there. What we didn't know, however, was the exact lay of the land at the head of that basin. Instead of a gradual slope, it turned out that we were walking in a steep canyon that slowed our progress and shrouded our view. At first light, we could only see parts of the parks above us. And by the time we got to the place where the elk were, the time was long past when the elk would be there.

The hunting country we were in looked good enough, however. There was a creek, rolling grassy benches, and black timber up above the open parks. With that kind of layout, there was little doubt the elk had moved up into that timber to spend the day. So we followed them and split up to go through the timber. It was in that thick cover that I jumped a bunch of elk. When they ran, I ran after them. Within fifty yards, they stopped to see what was

Glassing during the last hours and minutes of daylight will help you discover which parks the elk are using. Michael H. Francis photo.

If you can pick up the pattern that the elk are using, you can plan an ambush to take advantage of your knowledge. Michael H. Francis photo.

coming after them. I ended up shooting my elk at about twenty yards and then spent an entire day packing it out of that drainage.

If finding elk later in the season after they've felt hunting pressure makes it more difficult to spot them, there's some consolation in the fact that a hunter usually has snow to help him along by then. Snow on the ground allows a hunter to read the tracks elk leave behind in those openings.

If your binoculars or spotting scope is good enough, you can see beds and the meandering paths that elk make when they feed. You can see the places where elk paw the snow to get at the grass underneath. Or, you may be able to spot the tracks that hunters leave behind and know which areas to avoid because they are being hit exceptionally hard.

The important thing is to use your optics and do your scouting if you plan to hunt the open parks and meadows. To do this may take some fine-tuning on your part depending on the type of area you plan to hunt. Open parks on east-facing slopes, for example, will get dark earlier in the evening than those on west-facing slopes which catch the last sunlight of the day. Those east-facing parks may require scouting during the morning hours. Or, you may find that elk come out in them earlier in the evening.

In the same vein, you may find that elk stay out longer in the morning on west-facing parks because it takes longer for the sunlight to warm them.

Depending on your area, you have to decide the most productive time to do your scouting. Then you have to learn the morning or evening pattern that will best suit your hunting tactics so you can take advantage of your knowledge.

Hunting the open parks and meadows can be productive, if you go about it with the knowledge and patience of a veteran elk hunter. To do that, the first thing you have to know is that elk are in those openings for one reason and one reason alone. They're sneaking around in them to feed, not to soak up the sunshine, admire the moonshine, or make themselves vulnerable to the veteran elk hunter—you.

Elk Hidey Holes

There is a time, after the opening week muzzle blasts cease to echo through the canyons, that all elk seem to disappear. You can't find them anywhere.

Hunters look in the open parks and meadows which were their night-time playgrounds in the weeks before the season started. They look to the migration paths where the snows and cold of oncoming winter will force the elk to travel. They look to the winter range, summer range, and seemingly everywhere . And still, there are no elk to be found.

The time has arrived for elk to seek the hidey holes within their home range. It's the time for them to hide out, stay put, play it safe, and increase their chances of surviving to see another day.

Now, you can ask your wildlife professionals about the term hidey holes and it's not likely that they're going to recognize the expression. From them, you'll hear terms like elk security cover. But hidey holes has always been the term I used. Maybe it's because that's just what these things are to me, holes within the exterior boudaries of an elk's home range. And they're certainly great places to hide. In fact, the knowledgable hunter has to choose the hidey holes well that he plans to hunt because there are many that are just too tough, either to get into yourself, or get an elk out of if you happen to shoot one there.

The way these hidey holes develop into a place where elk hide out is simple enough. Elk don't like to run into hunters with blazing guns. They don't like to see hunters stalk them either. And the mere presence of so many humans in the woods is enough to make elk edgy and push them toward places where they will be left alone.

Once pushed by hunters, the elk move to a new area until they are pushed out of there. They move again, and again are pushed out. This process tends to take up the first days of the elk season until the animals finally find areas where no hunter pushes them out. These areas are hidey holes.

As a result, the hidey holes basically mean two things to the elk hunter. They are places elk hide. They are also places where other hunters don't go in search of elk. That last piece of information is the one an experienced elk hunter learns to rely on. That's because it's far easier to predict what other hunters will do than to try to predict where an elk might be hiding.

The thing to do is prepare something of a personality profile of an elk hunter and apply it to the country you plan to hunt. Open parks and ridges? Yes, the hunters do flock there. Wide-open southern slopes? Yes, the hunters are there, too. Places with good access for hunters on foot and horseback? Yes, it's just the same. Almost all areas close to a public road? Yes, they're almost all hunted hard. All these places provide reasonable access to hunters and are relatively easy to hunt. For that reason, after the first few days of the elk season, the elk are rarely there.

To find elk, look to the more difficult spots to hunt. They can take on many forms. North-facing slopes tight with cover? That's a good bet. Those jungles of deadfall where you spend as much time walking on logs as you do on the ground? That's a hidey hole too. The places a few miles and then a few more miles past the end of the road. Once again, it's a great place to look.

In the past, when there were fewer elk hunters and their modes of transportation were more primitive, it was a lot easier to find these elk hidey holes. If you just pushed a bit further into the back-country than other hunters, there were plenty of places for elk to escape the crush of orange-clad hunters. But that's changed in recent years. Hunters now have the help of four-wheel drive vehicles. More and more logging roads are being punched into country that you previously had to make long hikes to reach. There are more hunters using horses now. There are trail bikes and four-wheelers and snowmobiles. All of these things have helped hunters to invade country that the elk used to have to themselves.

These days, hunters have to be prepared to hike many miles to get past the crowds. They have to equip themselves well enough to stay back there for a few days or a few weeks. And, even when they're there, they have to be ready to walk into some unbelievable tangles in which other hunters in the area fear to tread.

One of the best ways to find hidey holes is to look for natural barriers. These will stop other hunters, or at least slow up their flow to the point that there might be an elk lurking somewhere behind them. These natural barriers might be nothing more than an area of deadfall that must be traversed to reach a more open area behind them or inside them. They might be a series of rocky cliffs. Or, they could be a swift-running creek or river. The more barriers like these that you put between yourself and the other hunters, the more likely it will be that you'll find a spot with enough solitude to hold an elk.

I had just such a place some years ago that I liked to hunt for deer and elk. There were no good horse trails into the area and even hunters on foot had a good deal of trouble getting in. It was too far to reach on foot from one side. From the other, a hunter had to go up over an extremely steep ridge and drop down the other side. I chose the ridge side and once I got over it, I had the area to myself. If there was a problem with this, it was that when a hunter downed game, it was just as tough to pack it out. You ended up doing it on your back on a pack frame and, as any hunter who has packed elk out this way will tell you, it's far from an easy task.

In my younger days, I really didn't care about the extra effort. I reveled in having the hidey hole to myself. But as I got older, the packing became more and more of a limiting factor to my going there. As time passed and I unraveled the trail system in my hidey hole, I finally found a good trail that would provide entry to a man on a horse. With that, my packing problems were gone. My secret spot was even better now that I had those problems solved. And I guarded the secret as well as I could, taking more than a few deer and elk out of the area. The trouble is that a horse leaves tell-tale tracks and eventually, someone else decided to follow those tracks. Over the years, more and more people found my trail and when enough of them did, the area's status as a hidey hole gradually diminished. It doesn't hold near the number of deer and elk now that it did in the old days.

Once an area becomes a regular hunting spot for many hunters, the elk move on to find another place where they won't be bothered. But even if relatively few hunters know about the spot, you'll never know if someone else has moved through the area an hour or two ahead of you. If a hunter is ahead of you, your chances of finding game are greatly reduced. So you just have to scout a little more and uncover new hiding places.

It should be pointed out that some hidey holes are not in the backcountry. Some hidey holes are hidden right out in plain view of hundreds of hunters. But there is usually some other factor that keeps elk hidden there.

A friend once described a patch of timber on a mountain slope that had hunters prowling all around it, yet few hunters ever stepped inside. The reason was that the patch of timber was alternately so tangled with deadfall and so choked with doghair pine, that it was tough for a hunter to walk through it. Even when a hunter did get inside, his ability to see was limited by the thickness of the cover. But if a hunter slowly worked his way through that patch of jungle, used his binoculars to penetrate the underbrush, and had his mind and body prepared to see elk at any moment, he just might take a bull out of there. My friend had taken several, yet in all the trips through that patch of thick cover, he had never come across another human track.

Another way to take advantage of hidey hole situations is to know where the elk will move when they're being pushed around by hunters who do venture into these areas. I had an uncle who was fairly heavy-set and couldn't cover the miles in the mountains the way many of us could. It was just too much work for him. His favorite approach was to let other hunters do the driving for him and to wait in ambush for the elk. These drivers weren't anyone he knew. They were just people out walking and scouring the drainages for elk and moving them around.

Over the years, my uncle had located a spot where the elk moved from one drainage to another in search of a hiding place. It was up a creek drainage about three miles, where two forks came together and there was a small opening on the hillside bordered with dark timber on each side. My uncle would hike in to that spot and then spend all day watching the hillside. He might not get an elk there the first day. He might not the next. But at some point during the season, an elk would cross in search of a new hiding place and my uncle would down him. He took an elk there every year.

It's interesting to note that my uncle preferred hunting weekends. That's because there would be more hunters out in the woods on those days, moving the elk around. It should also be noted that my uncle had done his homework in finding that spot, knowing that elk would move through there when they were pressured. By walking out the area, he learned the elk's travel routes and planned his hunt accordingly. By hunting elk all those years, he knew what elk would do. It was a matter of knowing the animals and doing the legwork first. Then and only then did that knowledge pay off for him in elk steaks every year.

The more typical hidey holes hold elk because they're just too tough to hunt or to get game out of once you get it on the ground. To me, the definitive hidey hole was one that I found and checked for several years, but one in which I never downed an elk. This place had several things going for it. It was camouflaged. It was

There are places tucked away in elk country where the bulls go to hide during periods of great pressure. Bob Krumm photo.

remote. It was tough to hunt. And, getting game out of it would have been nearly impossible.

This one was located clear up near the top of a mountain and was blocked off by shale rock and cliffs. From a distance, it didn't look like there was enough cover there to hold an elk or enough area in which it could have survived. But once you climbed up to the area, it was gorgeous. There was a timbered bench and a nice open park at the bottom of a draw. They had food, cover, and water all in the same spot.

I discovered the spot would hold elk one day when I was glassing other areas with my spotting scope and happened to look over at the bench and saw some tracks. I followed the tracks in the snow and they led me to a dandy six-point bull. I watched the big bull off and on that year, but never went up after him. The next year, I glassed again and saw a big bull again, possibly the same one. I told myself that one of these years, I was going to have to go after him, but that year my tag was already filled. When I got back to town, I told a friend about the spot and that from

With hunters penetrating further and further into elk country, there are fewer and fewer places elk can hide. Mark Henckel photo.

a distance, it looked like there was a huge bull up there. It was a week later that my friend reported back. He said he had gone up there and was coming down the slope when he cut some elk tracks made by a cow and a calf. With a cow permit in his pocket, he fired when he caught up with the pair, but missed. It was in following up the shot, however, that his eyes were really opened. When he saw the steep and rugged country that the elk had escaped into, he said he was happy he had missed. Even if he had shot an elk there, he never could have gotten it out.

In further examinations of the area, this hidey hole turned out to be the best form of protection a big bull could ever have. For one thing, the elk only pulled into there when the snows were piled deep. It was impossible for a hunter to get a horse in the area. There was thick deadfall in the timber. The open slopes were exceptionally steep. And the area was protected by rocky cliffs almost all the way around.

The area was so tough, in fact, that if you did shoot an elk in that spot, you'd have to eat him on the spot. For that reason, it was a place where elk go and stay. And, as far as I'm concerned, they can continue to go and stay there forever because I'm not going in after them. If they have to go to that much of an extreme to escape hunters, they'll escape me, too. If you've ever tried to get one out of a place like that, you'll know why.

In the end, it's just this type of hidey hole that may be the salvation of elk in the West. As time goes by, the number of hunters is increasing and the ability of those hunters to penetrate the back-country is improving as well. Many of the old hidey holes have disappeared. New ones are not to be found everywhere. If for no other reason than it stops the mechanized advance into elk country, designated wilderness areas do offer some protection for the elk and the hidey holes within them. In places without designated wilderness, there are going to have to be hidey holes so rough and rugged and inaccessible and miserable that hunters can't get into them or take an elk out if there's to be any chance for elk to survive.

Some might call it an odd twist of fate that often the only place to find an elk between the opening of the season and the onset of winter is in the most miserable places in the mountains. But it's a testament to a great species that these animals can live in these places, move around in them with relative ease, and even

Often, there is a barrier like a river or steep ridge, that stops hunters and creates a place with some security for elk. Michael H. Francis photo.

thrive in their harsh environments while hunters cannot. In these hidey holes blessed with food, water, and cover, the elk can live comfortably, out of the reach of hunter's guns. And if the hunters want elk badly enough, they'll seek out these hidey holes, go in after the elk, and pay the price for their journey.

But just as I said before, tread carefully in the hidey holes and take a firm grip on your conscience before you pull the trigger. It's one thing to down an elk in these places. It's quite another to pack them back to civilization with the meat still fresh and fit for the dinner table.

A hunter should always remember that reaching the first of these goals without the second is the hollowest of victories. And it's attained only at the expense of a great animal which deserves a better fate from those who join him in his hidey holes during the toughest times of elk season.

Is It Really Just Dumb Luck?

Early on in my elk hunting career, when elk and how to hunt them seemed more like a mystery than anything I would be able to master, I happened upon a hunter who found success every year. It was a chance meeting far back in the timber as I was working

There always seem to be some hunters who do everything wrong and still luck into a big bull elk. Michael H. Francis photo.

a mountain slope to the north and he was waiting for partners coming in from another direction.

Standing there in the timber, we talked about our hunting that year and in years past. The other hunter, obviously a seasoned veteran of countless years in elk country, told me he had his job back in town worked around to the point that he could take an entire month off during the hunting season. And each year, at some point in time, he found himself looking down his gun at a legal elk.

After sharing my misfortunes with him in trying to do the same thing, I finally asked him how much luck he figured was involved in getting an elk. His reply was that it was about ninety-nine percent.

That answer was hardly comforting. And, I've learned since that it wasn't necessarily true.

Beginning elk hunters often wonder just what it's going to take to get an elk. Even some hunters who have been at it for many years have gone through some almost unbelievable dry spells. Yet it sometimes seems like certain hunters were born under a lucky star with the way they take elk under circumstances that don't seem to produce for other hunters.

But the truth of the matter, and a fact that veteran elk hunters know, is that after a while, a hunter goes a long way in making his own elk hunting luck.

It's true, elk will often appear as if by magic. You look. And look. And look some more. Day after day after day. And just about the time you're positively sure that there isn't an elk within miles of where you're hunting, that your tag will never be filled, and that you'd better trade your gun in on a set of golf clubs, an elk magically appears. Often, the elk is just standing there in the timber, not even very far away, and you wonder why you hadn't seen him there before.

There's really no explanation for the phenomenon that seems to dictate that after you've finally given up, the elk finally give in. But it can happen that way. Even to the veteran hunters.

One of my favorite complaints in this regard was told to me by an elk hunter who had just put in a solid week of hard hunting without seeing so much as a single elk hair that was still growing on an elk. He finally confided to me that as far as he knew, the elk were finally in cahoots with the bears in that particular mountain range. The bulls and cows had sold out some calves to the bears in return for safe hiding places during the hunting season. The bears, in turn, had dug extra dens over the course of the summer. When elk hunting season arrived, the elk had hidden out in the holes and the bears had kicked the dirt in over the top of them and neatly covered the dirt with leaves and pine needles so the whole area looked natural again. That way, hunters like him couldn't find the elk and wouldn't be able to spot the holes either. It was the only logical reason the hunter could come up with to explain why elk hunting could be so poor.

While the elk being in cahoots with the bears is always something to watch out for, it's more likely that hunters have a heavy influence on their own success or failure in their search for elk. The longer a hunter is at the game and the more he tries to improve his skills, the more likely it is that the little things he has learned along the way will play an increasing role in helping him along.

A beginning hunter, for example, may head into the elk woods with hard-soled boots that give away his presence with every step. A veteran hunter knows the value of footwear that allows him to move quietly and won't settle for anything else when it's time to buy new boots.

Knowledge of the animals and what they do will overcome the need for luck. Michael H. Francis photo.

A novice hunter will walk through elk country without paying much attention to the sounds around him or will pass off every chirping sound as being made by birds. A hunter with experience knows he has to listen closely because the calls of the often-vocal calf elk sound very much like those of birds. The big difference is that the birds are likely to just have other birds nearby. The calf may give away the position of a whole herd of elk, bulls included.

If you're new at the game, you often feel that if you just cover enough ground in the mountains, eventually you'll bump into an elk and fill your tag. While covering a lot of distance is definitely one school of thought in elk hunting, it can be far more important to know when to go slow and to look country over thoroughly. Though elk will cover a lot of ground over the course of the year, there are some areas where they will hold for long periods of time and other places they simply wander through. There are certain places that elk seek out at certain times of the year, as well, while other spots are reserved for other weeks or months on the elk's internal calendar. And there are certain hiding spots that elk will seek out when pressured by hunters. A veteran simply knows what these high quality areas look like.

As a hunter gains experience, he also knows what kind of demands he's going to put on his equipment. If there's the likelihood that he's going to have to take three-hundred-yard shots with his rifle, the hunter will know how his bullet is going to perform at that distance and how he'll have to hold his point of aim. That hunter will have the optics at his disposal to be able to spot and positively identify the type of elk he's looking for at that distance.

If horses are part of his hunting scheme, he'll know how to handle them. If he hunts with a backpack and sets up a spike camp, he'll know what he needs to take along and what he needs to leave at home. Or if he hunts from his vehicle, he'll know the gear that will be stored in his day pack or fanny pack so that he can comfortably track elk all day and won't perish in the darkness if he has to endure an unplanned overnight stay in the mountains.

Most important of all, the veteran elk hunter is likely to know his hunting country on an intimate basis. He'll have done his homework with topographic maps and spent the time scouting the area on foot both in and out of hunting season. He'll know the feeding areas, bedding areas, and the trails in between. The veteran will have learned elk movements both when the animals are at peace in the mountains and when they're spooked.

These are the pieces of the elk hunting puzzle that beginners are just starting to accumulate. They're learning with each new experience in elk country and each contact with a veteran elk hunter who learned it himself over the years.

There's really no timetable that dictates that when you pass a certain point you've become a veteran elk hunter. There's no set period of time it takes. There's no graduation ceremony where you can pat yourself on the back that you've finally made it. All the time in the mountains and the experience you gain in and out of the field goes toward that end, however. It's a goal that every elk hunter who is really serious about the game hopes to attain some day.

The claim by that veteran hunter that getting an elk is ninety-nine percent luck doesn't really take any of these factors into account. And, frankly, that hunter may not have thought about all the little things that go into finding consistent success in pursuit of elk. But these little things can and do add up.

One factor that the veteran hunter did have in his favor however, was to put in plenty of time in the elk woods every year. He spent a solid month out there, learning things all along the way and, if need be, giving luck a chance to work things out for him. That certainly was to his advantage.

The thing that all elk hunters must remember, whether they're veterans already or simply hope to be some day, is that while luck can play a role, it's a poor bet to count on it helping you.

There will always be the hunter who cuts his hunting short one day, decides to sit around camp, and has a six-point bull wander within range of his easy chair while he sips on a cup of freshly-brewed coffee.

There will always be the hunter who gets up late, drives toward the trailhead long after sun-up and picks up an easy elk off the road while you see nothing despite a long hike in the darkness to get to some distant meadow at first light.

And, there will always be the hunter who couldn't hit the broad side of a barn while sighting in his rifle, yet pulls off a miraculous three-hundred-yard-plus shot at a big bull streaking through the trees at full tilt and drops the elk in its tracks.

For some reason, Lady Luck holds a special place in her heart for these nimrods. Somehow, some way, they get more than their share of elk in every season, in every state that elk call home.

But if you're looking for consistent success without having to rely too heavily on Lady Luck playing a leading role, you can always rely on the lessons that elk hunting teaches the hunter who really wants to learn. In time, they'll get their share of elk, too. In time, they'll realize that they've finally become veteran elk hunters themselves. And who knows, they may get so good at the game, that they can even find those bear holes where all the elk go to hide when no one else in elk country can find them.

■

ADVANCED TACTICS

To this point, the elk hunter has built much of his learning on the shoulders of others. Hunters who came before him have imparted the tactics that have led him to his elk. His job has been one of learning and adapting that knowledge to his own particular patch of elk country.

Now is the time for the elk hunter to strike out on his own. If anything, this is his creative stage. It's not enough to just hunt elk in the traditional methods. He must branch out and explore new territory in the game of elk hunting. He must make his own mark and begin to tackle new challenges.

This is where the elk hunter uses his creativity to go beyond the past, while paying homage to some of the traditions of the past that have served hunters well.

It's in this advanced stage of solving the elk puzzle that the hunter learns about items that are on the breaking edge of the sport. While hunters of the past talked only to the bulls during the rut, the hunter of today must learn to imitate cows and calves too, if he wants to reap the benefits of calling in all seasons. While other hunters have used scent on themselves to mask their own scent, the new breakthrough is scent spray misting which can even befuddle an elk that's directly downwind from you and bring him within range. There are zone hunting techniques that will help pinpoint the places you can find elk. And if you understand the basic principles behind moving elk used in the past, you can fit them to your own particular situation today.

While elk hunting is an old, old sport, it seems the new breakthroughs in tactics are coming at a rapid pace these days. The reason is that veteran hunters are becoming bolder and more aggressive in their approach and more innovative in their strategies.

With so many new things to help a hunter, does it somewhere become an unfair match of man against animal? And what new advances in technology are really too much for the elk to handle? That, I'm afraid, is a question that most hunters will have to answer for themselves. Until they decide, the experiments in advanced tactics will continue by elk hunters who make it this far down the trail. And as long as they keep experimenting, the face of elk hunting will be ever-changing.

Hunting the Zones

No one goes out side in a swim suit on a twenty-below-zero day. People don't purposely sit out in the sun if they know they're getting a bad sunburn. And if the whole area is abuzz with mosquitoes, they certainly don't try to help the little buggers along in getting their fill of a man-made meal.

It seems only logical that a person will do everything he can to make himself or herself as comfortable as possible. If not, there'd be no need for overstuffed chairs for living rooms or comfortable mattresses for people to sleep on. We wouldn't have warm clothes for winter and cool ones for summer. And we wouldn't spend near the money we do on things called modern conveniences.

Man, the animal, likes to be comfortable. For all the same reasons, elk, the animal, likes to be comfortable, too.

This basic sameness between man and elk is something that hunters too often ignore. They view an elk as something very different from man and make finding elk an almost mystical experience based on happenstance and luck. What they need to capitalize on instead is the sameness of needs of different animals.

The same things, in fact, can be said about all creatures. They

Elk will seek certain elevations at certain times of the year and hunting this elevation zone can lead you to an elk. Michael H. Francis photo.

all share the same basic needs. They need food, air, water, and a secure place to live. Find an area that has all these things and you'll find the animals you're after.

My own way of putting it is that you have to hunt the proper zone to put yourself in a position to see elk. In short, you do zone hunting. In the Rocky Mountains, that means you have to find the right elevation zone and the comfort zone within it where the elk are holding. Both the elevation zone and comfort zone go hand-in-hand.

Often, the elevation zone where you'll find elk is a seasonal factor. In the cold of winter, you'll find elk at generally low elevations. In the heat of summer, you'll find them up high. And during the months of autumn, when hunting seasons are going on, you might find them at either place or somewhere in between.

The comfort zones are found within the elevation zones. The comfort zones are places where the elk have abundant food, good water, and the right type of timber for security cover. Comfort zones might also hold mineral licks, wallows, or other key habitat ingredients.

Advanced Tactics

Within elevation zones, there are things like wallows that offer comfort for the elk in each specific season. Michael H. Francis photo.

It was during my bighorn sheep hunting years that I hit on the elevation zone theory. During that time, I did a lot of recording on maps. Whenever I saw a bunch of sheep, I marked the date and time that I saw them there. I didn't pay attention to what they were eating or where they were in relationship to water. All I wanted to know was when and where and what I saw. After several-hundred observations in all seasons, I had the elevation zones that the sheep preferred to be in. Just by looking back on my map, I could tell what elevation the sheep would be at during particular times of the year.

The same thing holds true for elk. It's a fair guess to say that elk will be at low elevations during the winter months. But that doesn't differentiate between the cows, calves, and young bulls that will be at the lowest elevations and the bigger bulls which will be just a bit higher on the mountain. For most hunters, it's the elevation zone of those older bulls that will help them along when the elk reach the winter ranges. The same type of information can be put to good use earlier in the season. If a hunter is looking for bugling bulls in September, the early gun season elk of October, or the migratory elk of November, there will be elevation differences that can be unraveled by simply observing elk and recording where you see them.

The next step is to find out the places within those elevations where the elk are likely to be. All a hunter has to remember is that elk are very much like we are. They're going to be in places where their basic life needs can be most easily met. Those elk need food, water and bedding areas that meet their basic comfort needs.

While elevation zones require actual physical observations to make them work, comfort zones can often be determined by scouting and map work. Once you find the elevation zone, you can read the sign within that area to locate the places where elk are moving to feed. You can look at the water courses in the area, locate the ponds, springs, wallows, and other places that the elk are using at that time of year.

When a person goes into a drainage and says he's never seen an animal there, it's for a reason. There's nothing in that drainage that the animal wants at that time of year. Elk may pass through it on their way to somewhere else where they're more likely to find more of the things they need.

Hunters should be aware, however, that elevation zones and comfort zones can be changed by external factors. Early, deep snows can move elk out of an area that they'd normally frequent during a certain part of the fall. Drought conditions might force animals to move, too.

One experience that comes to mind took place during just such a drought year. It was late in September, following a summer that dried up many streams and burned the grasses that normally grew lush in the high country. Without their normal sources of food and water, the elk were forced down into areas they'd normally move into only during the snowiest months of the year. The difference this year was that the alfalfa bottoms had withstood the long drought. While every other food source was withered and brown, those alfalfa bottoms shone like green emeralds against the drab hills around them. There was a stream down there, too, and a spring further up the slope on the way to some thick cover that served as a bedding area less than a mile away.

During most years, there are a few elk that stick in this country during the archery season and the first weeks of the gun season. But there usually aren't very many. This year, however, the area was loaded with elk. And even though the elk didn't match up to the elevation zone they should have been in, all the comfort zone factors were easily put in place. Helping the situation along, it was a time of year that the elk were bugling.

As a result, it was relatively easy to work within the elevation and comfort zones of the elk and locate them by their bugling. It turned out there were several good bulls in the area, among them a six-by-five bull that came within twenty-six yards of my calling position. That bull turned out to be a fine bow kill that was lured out of his bedding area while another mature bull was still bugling several hundred yards away.

Hunting the zones for elk is a skill that hunters will acquire only with years. It takes time to record enough elk sightings to learn the elevation zones elk are likely to be in at certain times of the year. It takes more time to unravel the maze of tracks and learn about feeding, watering, and bedding grounds within those zones.

Often, hunters don't even know what they've done in putting these pieces of the puzzle together. They just know if they go to a certain area, at a certain time of the year, at a certain time of the day, they seem to bump into elk every time. The reason is that the hunter has recorded facts in his mind that consistently lead him to elk. Yet he thinks it's just his good place to hunt year after year after year.

Those who know about zone hunting can approach it a little more scientifically than just relying on memory and going back to the same spot every year. By marking locations on a map and studying the areas around them, a hunter can piece together the lifestyles of elk throughout the hunting season. That kind of information offers a tremendous insight into the times and places that a hunter can expect to find elk. Then, at any point during the season, he can pick the time and place that are most likely to end up with a bull being taken and tagged. And people will correctly say that this hunter can go out and get an elk anytime he wants.

Cow Talk and Bull Talk

No one really knows the name of the first hunter who tried to communicate with elk. That event, I'm afraid, is so far back in time that there's just no record of it. But it's a sure bet that whoever it was, he was in for a shock.

In a way, I can almost picture it. It's early autumn and the aspen leaves have turned a brilliant yellow. In the chill of the early morning, a bull elk bugles. The hunter, sitting on a rock with his bow or spear by his side, hears the sound and decides to imitate it. But no sooner does that high-pitched whistle leave his throat than the bull answers back. Surprised, he makes the sound again. And this time, the bull comes charging in, bellowing his challenge, tearing big chunks out of the earth with his flailing antlers, and then just standing there glancing back and forth with a wild look in his eyes.

The first hunter to witness this scene was undoubtedly awe-struck by it. And hunters today, who have the same thing happen to them, are affected the same way.

Hunters can tell you that it's sheer excitement to call a big turkey gobbler within range. They can talk about the hiss of set wings as a flock of mallards or Canada geese makes their final descent toward decoys. And they can even talk about rattling in a big whitetail buck in the weeks of November.

But believe me, those are small potatoes when compared to an eight-hundred- to one-thousand-pound bull elk storming into view, shaking the trees with his antlers and roaring out his challenges to all comers. To have that wild-eyed monster raking the earth with his antlers. To have him closing in to within a few yards of you. And to hold your aim steady for a rifle or bow shot has likely brought more hunters to their shaking and quaking knees than any other experience in pursuit of fish and game.

It's no wonder then that each year, more and more hunters are exploring the strategy of using calls to bring elk within range of their gun, bow, or camera. It's a centuries-old form of excitement that hasn't been diminished a bit by the passage of time.

That doesn't mean, however, that the art of calling in elk hasn't changed over time. In recent years especially, just the opposite is true. Elk calling has been a dynamic force in the hunting world. And even though we have increased our knowledge dramatically,

Using a cow call has helped hunters to lure bulls, cows, and calves into bow or gun range in all seasons. Jim Hibbard photo.

one can't help but think that we're still just scratching the surface in terms of understanding all the facets of making elk sounds.

This language, which was dubbed Elk Talk in a book I did on the subject a couple of years ago, is a mixture of bull sounds, cow sounds, calf sounds, and some sounds which are common to all elk no matter what their age. It's in the use of this language that the real revolution in elk hunting has come. Like the coming of the centerfire rifle to replace the old muzzleloaders, it's a change that has made a huge difference to hunters taking to the field to hunt elk.

For most of recorded time, however, the only elk sounds that hunters knew anything about was the challenge call that bulls make during the rut in September and October. This call, which consists of a high-pitched squeal ending in a series of grunts, is made by bulls to establish their territories and defend their harems against other bulls that might be in the area. Because those bulls were defending the rights and properties they thought were their own, hunters imitating another bull encroaching on their territory would often lure the real thing into range. They used whistles, plugged pieces of hose, rifle shells, and even curled pieces of corrugated pipe to imitate the high-pitched whistle of breeding-time bulls.

It should be noted that hunters blowing through these things scored well on elk. All they made was a high-pitched whistle, but that was close enough to the real thing to work, just as long as the bull was really hot. In this elk hunting game, you had to be at the right place, at the right time, if you were going to bring in a bull. As a result, the hunter spent much of his time going from drainage to drainage trying to locate a hot bull. If the bulls he found weren't red hot, the hunter was out of luck.

As time went on, imitating the bugling bull with a call became more refined. Hunters found out that if they strained their vocal cords while inhaling through a tube, they could do the short squeals and grunts that went on the end of the shrill bugle. Using these grunt tubes were tough on the throat, but for hunters that could use them, they were a big advantage in bringing in elk.

Calls came on the market with internal reeds that claimed to do the same thing. Others came on the market with external reeds. And, finally, there was a dramatic breakthrough with diaphragm calls, the kind that turkey hunters were using to lure in gobblers.

Elk have a language all their own and they use it extensively to communicate with other elk. Michael H. Francis photo.

The diaphragm calls were a breakthrough, because for the first time, they really allowed a hunter to make the full range of elk noises in the bugle. You could do the squeal. You could do the grunts. You could do anything and everything that a bull could do. But they were tough to use. It often took hunters months of trying to perfect their calls. Some hunters, with gag reflexes that rebeled when any foreign object was placed in their mouth, couldn't use them at all. Yet the diaphragm call was a significant development.

As they got more familiar with the diaphragm calls, hunters made a wide variety of elk sounds with them. They could sound like bulls. They could sound like cows. They could sound like calves. For the most part, however, hunters didn't know what power they had.

It brings to mind the stories that Vince Yannone, a good friend and extremely successful elk hunter from Helena, Montana, would tell me. He said that long after the rut was done, he could bring in elk if he made this certain noise. The bulls wouldn't come in fast. They wouldn't answer back either. But you could pull them in even during the snow and cold of November if you only made this certain elk sound. And you could pull them in from some great distances as one back-tracking experience showed him. After shooting a five-point bull, he followed its tracks back for about a mile until he found the bed where the bull had been lying before the call roused him.

Other hunters had been making those noises too, but it wasn't until I invented and patented the Cow Talk call and put it out on the market that most hunters were introduced to it. Then the video cassette, *How to Talk to the Elk,* with Gordon Eastman, and *Elk Talk,* the book, where released to show how to make Cow Talk work for them. These things showed that there was much more to the language of elk than just the rutting-time bugle. And these other sounds would bring in elk all through the year, not just during September and October when the animals were hot enough to come in to any bull sound.

As we've explored the situation since then and paid more attention to the full range of elk sounds, we've found that there is much about calling elk that we've learned and much we still don't know.

A bull, for example, actually makes at least three kinds of calls. One of them is the challenge call that hunters have been hung up on for years. Another is a softer, high-pitched squeal which doesn't have the intensity of the challenge call, but is used instead to actually bring in the cows. In using that call, he brings in other bulls, too, to investigate just what he has in terms of female companionship. And the final one is the call he uses to communicate with other elk in all seasons, the way we make small talk and casual conversation with other humans.

That last call is the one common to all elk, though it may take on different pitches and be shorter or longer in duration depending on the age of the animal. The sound itself is something of a combination of a high-pitched chirp and a mewing sound. In younger elk, if you had to spell it, the sound would be something like ee-uh. In older elk, cows and bulls alike, it would be more of an eee-ow.

If you're lucky enough to hear a group of elk communicating with each other, however, you're likely to hear a wide variety of sounds. The higher-pitched sounds we've come to call calf sounds. The lower-pitched sounds are called cow sounds. But judging the age of elk through the sounds they make is a risky business indeed. I've heard three-year-old elk make those high-pitched calf sounds. And I've seen six-point bulls make the noises that people call cow sounds. The thing to remember is that these are sounds that all elk make and no matter how different your variation of those notes may be, they're saying the same things to the elk.

If there's a problem to be faced, it's that we really don't know what cow talk is actually saying to elk. In some instances, it seems be saying, "We're all over here." Other times, it's more like, "Everything is okay." And on still other occasions, it seems to say, "Come on over big boy, I'm in the mood for love." Whatever it's saying, however, it's potent medicine for the rifle-toting elk hunter as well as the bowman.

While it's anyone's guess as to what cow talk is saying to elk, it does appear that the old-time elk hunters were on the right track with their high-pitched whistles. That's because if there's one common denominator among all the sounds that elk make, it's high-pitched sound frequencies.

In a way, that's only logical. When you're hunting elk during the rut and you hear a faraway bugle, all you can hear is the high-pitched squeal. When bulls are trying to gather their cows, it's a high-pitched sound again. And if you listen to the first note of cow and calf sounds, that too is high-pitched.

For my own part, I learned just how high-pitched the cow and calf calls were more than four years ago when I was first developing the prototypes of the Cow Talk call. At the time, friends would ask me to blow the calls into the phone so they could hear what they sounded like. In every case, the high-pitched first note of the call would disconnect the phone. To my way of thinking, that high-pitched sound was so high that it was beyond the hearing range of humans, but well within that of the elk and other animals. How else could you explain the fact that the Cow Talk call would work on such a wide variety of wildlife including whitetails and mule deer, antelope, black bears, grizzly bears, coyotes, moose, mountain lion, and a variety of birds.

But the biggest magic in the call is the way it works on elk. But here too, we're still learning.

We've known, for example, that by mixing cow sounds with bull sounds during the rut, we stand a much better chance of calling a bull within shooting range than in the past when we used bull sounds alone. We also found out that the balance between bull and cow sounds should run heavily toward the cow sounds because a cow was what that bull was looking for. But we're still doing some fine-tuning. One thing we've learned could go a long way toward solving an elk caller's nemesis, the bull that comes in a distance only to hang up and stop before he comes within range. Elk callers have been plagued by this reluctant bull behavior ever since they first used a call. But in the cow call, we finally find an answer for the reluctant bull.

If there is more than one hunter in the group, send one hunter a distance toward the bull, while the other callers maintain their position. Then have the forward hunter make a single cow call and have him be ready for instant action. What's happened more times than it hasn't is that the bull has come charging in on the forward man, giving him an almost immediate shot. The logical reason is that the bull must figure that a lone cow has split off from the rival's herd and all he has to do is race in and steal her away. This strategy is most effective if there are two or more hunters in the group, because the bull will get the idea the herd has split up simply because of the different calling positions. If you're all alone, you'll have to advance and make the cow call yourself. It won't necessarily work all the time, but even if it works a fraction of the times a bull gets hung up, it is a tactic well worth trying.

That willingness to try new strategies, in the end, is the problem that traditional hunters face most often when deciding whether or not to use something like the cow call. In the past, calling was also so much a domain of the September-October bowhunter or rifleman that it was hard to convince hunters later in the season to use it. The guides and outfitters who had the early prototypes would invariably wait until all their tried-and-true elk hunting methods would fail before falling back on the call.

They'd spook elk in the timber and have them beyond the reach of their hunters before blowing on the cow call. And it would still stop elk.

Hunters would shoot at elk, miss, and start them running before the call would be blown. And it would still stop elk.

Sometimes, hunters would miss, start the elk running, stop them with the cow call, miss again, start the elk running, stop them with the cow call, miss again, and still have enough power in the call to stop the elk one more time.

Those who know anything about elk know that this kind of reaction is nothing short of pure magic. But from those experiences, we began to learn that the cow call seemed to work exceptionally well on animals that were under stress.

We also learned that the cow call gave us some flexibility in our more traditional hunting methods. For the rifle hunter able to reach long distances and down an elk in its tracks, the cow call would stop them for a standing shot. For the trophy hunter that would shoot only a record-class bull, the cow call would stop them so the hunter had a better chance to size up its antlers. And for the first-time elk hunter or the hunter getting up there in years who needed a little more time to steady themselves, the cow call would hold elk so that these hunters could squeeze off a decent shot.

The cow call has been used this way so much, in fact, that many hunters don't even realize that it can be used to lure in elk, too. The reason for this is that most rifle hunters haven't had the benefit of this kind of calling power in the past. For them, the elk hunting game has been a moving experience where you walk until you spot an elk and then shoot it. You find them. They don't find you.

Using bull sounds and cow sounds at the right time will bring a bull in close for the hunter. Ron Shade photo.

But hunters who have the patience to sit or even to walk slowly through elk country might be surprised at the pulling power of the cow call. If you only get yourself into an area where you know there are elk, sit still, and work the call for a half-hour or more, you may just spot a good bull sneaking in quietly, bent on enjoying the company of the other elk he knows are there.

What the rifle hunter has to realize is that there's a new tool at his disposal that's well worth the risk of using. In a way, he has to forget the past when the only elk noises being made were challenge calls. And he has to embrace the new wave of elk hunting including the high-pitched squeals of the bull and the cow and calf sounds that elk make year-round.

Don't expect the transition to be an easy one. There's too much tradition working against it.

Go to any elk calling contest you choose and listen to the champions and you'll still find that the caller who makes the roughest, toughest challenge call is the one that's going to win. But when you hear him, realize that most bulls will run the other way if the caller makes that noise in the elk woods. During the rut, the real bulls aren't looking for an elk that's rough and tough. They want an easy opponent with just a high-pitched squeal who'll be easy to run off so you can take his cows without being threatened. And if you want to call elk in at any other time during the year, try the cow and calf sounds for the many things they say to an elk.

For rifle hunters to fully understand these things and have faith in their new-found calling abilities, it's going to take some time. If you go to any camp of dyed-in-the-wool rifle hunters, you won't hear much talk about calling. For these hunters, it's been too many years of mornings in the open parks, afternoons in the black timber, and evenings spent scouting that have produced the most bulls over the years. For them, your first shot is often your only shot and no amount of blowing on a call is going to change their minds that you can't stop an elk that's been shot at and missed. There just hasn't been a lifelong tradition of elk calling to change their minds.

But go to any camp of elk callers who have suffered the past frustrations of bugling to elk in the rut only to have them run off in front of them, time after time after time, and you may hear something different. It's these hunters who have changed their calling strategies with the times, that may tell you about the new generation of cow and calf talk and the things it does in all seasons. They'll use hard words like revolutionary, magical, mystical, and unbelievably effective.

It's these hunters who know of cow talk and bull talk and when to use them. And it's these hunters who are well on their way toward becoming experts in the elk hunting world, simply because their methods of calling have kept up with the times.

Dollars and Scents

Bull talk is the venerable veteran of the elk hunting world. It's very likely been around for centuries. And, if done at the right time of year, it has helped many a hunter hang his tag on an elk. Cow talk is the new kid on the block and over the past few years, it too has made its mark by luring elk within range or stopping them from running out of the range of hunters' rifles. Both of these techniques rely totally on fooling an elk's ears, befuddling one of the senses that the animals rely on to protect themselves.

But if fooling just one of the senses brings results, what happens if you try to fool two senses? What happens if you also negate the elk's powerful sense of smell as well as his hearing? Wouldn't that be doubly effective? The answer is yes, it certainly does, but only if you know how.

Just as using cow and calf sounds was a revolutionary and devastating concept when it was introduced a few years ago, using an elk scent system is the breakthrough of today. Its results can be equally unbelievable as scenting once again rewrites the rules of elk hunting.

Using scents to pursue and take animals in itself is hardly new. Trappers have been using them for years to attract animals and put them in the exact position that they want them. White-tailed deer hunters have also used doe-in-heat scents to enhance their chances. They've laid scent trails through buck country and relied on the deer's noses to lead them into ambush situations. And, cover scents have also been explored extensively. You can buy them to mask human odor with such aromas as pine scent, dirt scent, apple scent, whew!...skunk scent, fox scent, elk scent, deer scent and a virety of other smelly things.

The biggest problem with using scents in the past has been that

Elk will often use their nose to detect the scent left behind by other elk that have moved through the area. Michael H. Francis photo

they not only clog the nostrils of the animals you seek, but they clog your own nostrils as well. Or, if they were used in a scent trail, you had to make your drag trail first, then set up your ambush and sit and wait for the animals to come. Neither of these things favored the elk hunter. Because elk have such a strong smell themselves, you can use your nose to locate elk before you see them—if your nostrils aren't clogged. And because hunters usually end up covering a great deal of ground in search of elk, laying a quick scent trail and waiting in ambush isn't usually feasible.

In the book *Elk Talk,* I discussed an alternative to these scent systems that I discovered, called scent mist spraying. But there wasn't anything being sold on the market commercially to take advantage of the new scenting scheme. So since then, I put out something called Rocky Mountain Elk Scent and included a spray mist atomizing bottle with it. Using it involved saturating the air with elk scent while keeping yourself scent-free. That is accomplished by using an atomizer bottle, similar to the ones used to dispense perfume and cologne in a fine mist. An elk hunter uses the atomizer to dispense diluted cow-in-heat elk urine in a fine mist.

This misting system has produced some surprising results for

An atomizer bottle will send out a fine mist spray of water and cow urine to saturate the air downwind with elk scent. Mark Henckel photo.

the few hunters using it over the past couple of years. The first hunting heresy you have to be willing to accept, however, is that being upwind of the elk puts you in good position. In the past, being upwind and letting the elk get a whiff of you was the biggest no-no of all. It meant certain failure as the elk caught your wind and ran off. With the mist system, you want the elk downwind so they get a whiff of the elk scent.

To get ready to use the scent mist, you have to buy some cow-in-heat scent and get youself an atomizer bottle. Then, you mix the elk scent and water in the proper proportions. Straight elk scent is just too powerful to use by itself. So you dilute it in your atomizer bottle at a ratio of about six parts water to one part elk urine. The water produces the fine spray that carries the scent toward the elk while saturating the air.

The next thing you need to know is when and how to use it. The rule of thumb is to use it whenever you know or suspect elk are in the area. If the elk are coming toward you, like they would be in a bugling situation where you can keep track of the sounds of the bull, spraying the mist in the air will saturate the area downwind of you. Even if the bull is coming in from a different direction, they still almost always try to circle downwind of the caller to let their nose make the final determination on whether it's safe or not to come in close.

One of my earliest experiences with the misting system involved just that type of situation. It was late in the breeding season and I was using both bull sounds and cow sounds to bring a bugling bull within range. But that bull came on ever so slowly. It took more than an hour to reel in that bull and when he got close, he started that inevitable circling that would take him downwind of me. But this time when he got downwind, instead of getting that tell-tale man scent that would normally have ended the drama right there, he got a noseful of the cow-in-heat mist spray. The branch-antlered bull followed that scent in without hesitation, closing quickly to within twenty yards.

When the elk came in, I stayed low to the ground. In that position, I didn't make the upright silhouette of a man and presented no threat to him. Just to see what would happen, I waved my hand at the bull. At that, the animal bolted over the hill. I began cow calling and scenting again, however, and brought him back. Then I spooked him and called and scented him back again. It worked that way three times before the bull finally tired of the game.

Using the cow call and mist system together isn't just a potent combination during the rutting season, however. It seems to work well at any time of year.

During the month of August, I was working on a video called *The Art of Elk Hunting* with Gordon Eastman. At the time, when the bulls were still in velvet and the rut was still far off, I used the cow call and mist spray to approach a group of elk without the benefit of cover to help me. There was a strong wind blowing in their direction and I simply saturated that wind with mist while intermittently blowing on the cow call. Using the two together, I worked to within forty yards of the bunch and some of the elk moved toward me until the closest ones were ten to fifteen yards away. It made a powerful scene on the video and showed just how effective the mist spraying could be.

I accomplished the same thing on the winter range during the month of February. The elk, both bulls and cows, were put at ease by the sound of the cow call and attracted by the scent of the mist spray. This time, I was spraying the wind in front of a rock. And when I returned to the rock some time later, a group of bulls had actually surrounded it and were licking the rock to collect what they could of the spray that had settled there.

One final experiment with the atomizer took place before the season on a bunch of elk we were watching that came into an alfalfa field to feed every evening. We took my scent mixture and sprayed it on a fencepost at the entry point to the field and on the ground in two different spots nearby. When the elk arrived to go into the field to feed, the cows went right on by. But when the bull arrived, he ran right over to the fence post and started licking it. Then he searched out the other two spots where the scent was on the ground and lingered there. It showed me that the scent played a strong part in attracting a bull even when he was hungry and there was a field full of alfalfa that normally would have held his attention.

An elk call alone doesn't usually keep an elk from the important task of filling its belly. In a feeding situation, they'll often ignore all calls. But the scent opens up another avenue to get their attention and used in tandem with the calls, it can be a potent combination.

The notion that scents can play an important role in elk hunting

Elk rely on their noses to verify what their ears have heard or their eyes have seen to protect themselves from danger. Michael H. Francis photo.

shouldn't come as a big surprise to hunters. Long before the time when they become a veteran of the elk woods, their noses know the scent of elk well. It hangs in the air and is blown in the wind many times when elk are nearby. Elk bedding areas and even individual elk beds also hold the heavy and distinctive odor. And, just as long as your sense of smell isn't clogged with some other scent, a hunter learns to literally follow his nose because it very well could lead him to an elk.

The first thing a veteran elk hunter does when he smells elk is to check which way the wind is blowing. Sometimes, you can smell elk that are fifty to seventy-five yards away. As a result, if the hunter heads in the direction the wind is coming from and moves slowly, he can sometimes pick up the elk before they detect he's there. At times, those elk will be bedded down. Or, it could be an old elk bed itself near which an elk urinated before moving on. One of the keys to tell how far away the elk might be is to pay attention to the power of the wind as well as its direction. If there isn't any breeze, you may be awfully close to the source of that smell. If the wind is moderately strong, it may have carried the elk smell a greater distance.

The persistence of elk scent was brought home to me while teaching my son Ryan how to track. It was the opening day of the rifle season and we were following elk tracks in snow that was alternately crusted and soft on a north-facing slope. We jumped some elk, including a spike, and followed them for about an hour before we decided to give up on them and hunt our way back to the truck. Our path back took us along a finger ridge that often held a bull for a week or more some time during the course of the rifle season before it eventually pulled out of there.

In the course of our hunt along that ridge, I first spotted some old sign and then my nose caught the tell-tale smell of elk. I signaled to Ryan by touching my nose and we proceeded on slowly, ready to see elk at any moment, following our noses in the direction the smell was coming from. But instead of an elk, we found an old elk bed that was iced over and noticed the spot nearby where a bull had urinated before moving on.

The following weekend, we decided to hunt another area nearby. But our walking through that country eventually led us to the same finger ridge. This time, we came in from another direction and again picked up the smell of elk. Following the same routine of the week before, we pointed our noses in the direction of the smell and homed in on the source. It turned out that we came upon the same elk bed. Even though that bed was now well over a week old, the odor of that bull urine was still strong enough to strongly suggest that the elk himself was still there.

Even if the smell might lead you to nothing more than an old bed, it's something that still shouldn't be ignored. Even if elk are spooked and just move through an area, they'll often leave their scent on the wind. By following it up, you may be able to tell just how close or how far behind the elk you are and what your chances of catching up with them might be.

If the animals are running, you can determine if you spooked them yourself and get an idea of what might lie ahead. If the tracks are fresh and the elk are walking, you can follow them up, alert to the fact you might run onto the elk at any time. Or if the beds are fresh, you may have happened on the edge of a herd's bedding area and there could be more elk nearby.

When the smell and sign indicate that elk could indeed be close, it gives the hunter the opportunity to pull out his binoculars and really penetrate the timber to see if you can spot an elk up ahead. With those binoculars and the scent on the wind to guide you, you may see the odds and ends and pieces of elk that could add up to a bull. All of that is possible because you let your nose warn you that elk might be lurking in the vicinity.

Because your own nose is so important, I never put scent on myself even though there are many excellent cover scents available on the market. Instead, I try to eliminate my own odor as well as I can. To do that, I rely heavily on baking soda and baking soda mixed with water. In all but the harshest back country camps, it's possible to take a quick sponge bath in camp with a mixture of baking soda and water. Then I dash on baking soda in all the parts of the body that tend to perspire most.

For my clothes and equipment, I use one of the scent-eliminating sprays on the market. Most of these, too, contain some kind of baking soda base. And they help to mask or remove human odor on things that can't be washed as easily as your own body including your bow, backpack, shirt, and cap.

With my own scent down to a minimum, I can use my nose to locate elk that are upwind from me and use the mist spray system both to cover my own odor and provide a reason for the elk to come in that are downwind from me.

The atomizer approach is a powerful addition to the arsenal of the elk hunter at any time of the year, especially when used in combination with cow calling. It seems as if the elk have become so accustomed to relying on their noses as a defense system to back up their other senses, that once you get past their ability to smell danger, it's easy to get within range. It has been said that elk hear four times better than we do. No one knows how much better their sense of smell is than that of man.

As I said early on when we were doing our first experimenting with the scent mist spray system, there was only one reservation I had over letting other people know about it. It's such a deadly system at all times of the year when used together with cow calling, that it's going to make an awful lot of otherwise mediocre elk hunters perform like real experts when they go after elk.

Head'em off at the Pass

You can move elk anywhere they want to go. But if you try to move them somewhere else, you're in for a tough time.

For the most part, those two sentences tell a hunter all he needs to know about trying to push elk in a certain direction toward waiting hunters. It's not as easy a proposition as you might think. In fact, it's nothing that should be left to the novice if you're looking for sure-fire results. And even among the veterans, the results can sometimes be surprising.

One of my favorite elk hunting stories of all time is something I call "The Great Gallatin Elk Stampede of 1916." It involved just one of those maneuvers designed to move elk within range of waiting hunters. But this story has more. It has mystery, intrigue, night-time maneuvers, and even involved getting a game warden drunk.

The story was told to me by the lone survivor of the great stampede, Roy Walton of Bozeman, Montana. Walton was nineteen at the time, but was already an experienced elk hunter and expert horseman, having grown up in an age when knowing how to handle a horse was at least as important as knowing how to handle a rifle. And his story took place in the Gallatin River canyon of Montana, right on the northwest edge of Yellowstone National

Elk killed at Sunnybrook Camp Dec 6th 1916 Gallatin

The end result of the elk stampede of 1916 was an elk or two for every hunter in camp that year. Roy Walton photo.

Park, during the month of November.

Back in those days, elk hunters never went into the field until after election day. Walton's group was no different, packing in with horses and wagons to a spot known as Sunnybrook Camp, named for the whiskey that his uncle would bring along to camp from the hotel bar he operated back in town. Indeed, it was a different time than today. In order to reach camp, they often had to build bridges to cross the river. Once they got to camp, the main purpose was to bring home a supply of elk meat, preferably from some big, fat cow.

But the 1916 season wasn't smiling on the several dozen hunters that were working the upper Gallatin that year. They hunted for days without seeing even fresh sign of an elk. And when they finally did get some elk in the area, a pack of wolves moved in for the kill right near their camp. The wolves were so close to camp, in fact, that the hunters built fires near their horses to make sure the wolves would keep their distance. The following morning, many of the hunters rode after the wolves while the others salvaged what they could of the elk and loaded the meat in wagons to be taken back to Bozeman and be distributed to people who needed it. Though the hunters trailed those wolves all day, they never did catch up with them. And, their appearance didn't help out the elk hunting either.

After more days of seeing no elk, a plan was finally hatched to bring some elk within range of the hunters. It was certainly a bold plan by today's standards, but it had been done before by hunters in the area. A group of men would ride into Yellowstone National Park and herd the elk during the night out into the legal hunting area.

If there was a hitch to the plan, it was that the game warden and some personnel from Yellowstone were visiting the camp at the time. That did present a problem. But one of the better drinkers in the group was assigned the task of pouring the whiskey to them that night and getting them drunk. Meanwhile, late in the afternoon, nine horsemen took off for the park. Their job was to locate some elk and get them moving. Walton was one of the group that rode about five miles into Yellowstone and found a herd that would suit the hunters' needs.

As darkness fell, there was a herd of forty to fifty elk out in front of the men. And slowly, guided by miner's lamps on their foreheads, the men started riding back, moving the elk out in front of them. To hear Walton tell it, the job was relatively easy. The sight of those lamps panning back and forth in the darkness would keep the elk moving. As long as the line of riders was spread out behind them, the elk would keep going in the direction the men wanted them to go.

Through the clearings, the dark timber, up slopes and down, the men rode, hearing the sounds of the elk talking to one another out in front of them. When the miner's lamps played out, the riders continued on in the dark, being bumped on the head by limbs, scratched by trees, grabbed by brush, and generally worked over by the rugged country they were riding through. As far as they knew, the plan was working perfectly.

What the men didn't know was that their herd of forty or fifty elk was acting like an elk magnet as it walked through those mountains. Other bunches of elk were being picked up along the way, a few here, a few there, and many more than a few from some places.

It was just breaking dawn when Walton and the other riders drew near to the ambush spot just over the park line. The other hunters in the group had stationed themselves on the surroun-

Advanced Tactics ■

Roy Walton, who told the story of the stampede, was still in his teens when he took part in the event. Mark Henckel photo.

ding slopes, ready to take aim when the elk appeared. But when there was enough light to really see, neither the riders nor the men on the slopes could believe what was out there. The herd of forty to fifty elk had grown during the night-long ride into a herd Walton estimated at three thousand elk. There were elk everywhere.

Even now, Walton isn't sure what happened with that herd of three thousand elk, but something sure spooked them. Suddenly, the herd exploded and there were elk running in every direction. Part of the stampede raced back through the riders and Walton remembers elk brushing his legs on both sides. Other elk overran the hunters waiting on the slopes, to the point that those men were so busy scrambling for safety that they never fired a shot.

There was one man who fell asleep lying on top of a big sagebrush and awoke to find elk streaking past him on both sides. There was the tale of another man who was actually run over by the stampeding herd and lay flat on his back, pressed into the snow. When he came to, he looked over and there was a big calf nearby that had suffered a similar fate. Not wanting to come out of the ordeal empty-handed, the man grabbed his knife, and raced over there to get the calf. But about that time, the calf also came to and reared up, knocking the man down, and running over him again.

Walton said it took a while for the hunters to react to the situation. By that time, the main herd had raced down the valley out of sight. But there were still enough elk within range that the hunters did some damage. Walton recalls his own exploits of riding his horse at full speed alongside the running elk and shooting six of them by just tucking his saddle gun behind their shoulder and pulling the trigger. Other hunters shot enough elk that when the whole thing was over, there were enough elk on the ground for one or two for each of the men in camp. As Walton put it, there was enough for everyone, whatever they wanted.

After the shooting was done, Walton went back to his tent and crawled in his bedroll to get a little sleep. It was there that the now wide-awake game warden found him and demanded to know what had happened. And Walton, his clothes in shreds and his face covered with scratches from the night of riding through elk country in the dark, told the warden that he had no idea. He'd just been sleeping there all that time.

The herd of stampeding elk ended up running more than twenty miles down the Gallatin valley before they stopped. The elk hunters of Sunnybrook Camp caught up to them there several days later as they guided their wagons, now loaded with elk, back toward town. Along the way, they also encountered other hunters on the way in who had heard of the great number of elk that had suddenly appeared in the hunting area. They came in wagons similar to their own and in the new Model T's that were being used by more and more hunters who headed toward elk country.

While some of those late-arriving hunters got their elk, others among them got more than they bargained for when heavy snows that would have started the migration naturally descended on the area with a vengeance. There are tales of snow that measured seven feet on the level that buried the Yellowstone area during that storm. In fact, the snows were deep enough that many of those old cars were stranded in the backcountry by it. Those cars stayed there until the following spring, when the hunters went back in to retrieve them. But in the meantime, the mice had taken their toll on the cars, eating all the leather seats and dashboards, while the snow caved in the cloth tops.

It's a safe bet to say that stories like this one are unlikely to be repeated in this day and age. For one thing, hunters are much more likely to follow the game laws, respecting the sanctity of our national parks. For another, the drive to put meat on the table isn't nearly as strong as it was back then. And, finally, our attitudes toward wildlife like elk are much different now.

But the principles of pushing game toward waiting hunters is still basically the same. The riders were able to move those elk because they were pushing them in a direction they normally would go. The elk drive took them right down their normal migration path. The presence of the men behind the elk also provided just enough stimulus to get them moving. The riders didn't have to holler, beat drums, or make any other special noise. All they had to do was be there. As long as they were there, the elk would move.

The simple presence of man is enough to move elk within a drainage or move them completely out of it. One of the biggest mistakes that hunters make is to set up their camps too close to their hunting areas. Just the noises around camp will get on the nerves of elk that are anywhere within earshot. If they don't move out right away, they generally will move out within a matter of a day or less.

It used to be a common practice among some outfitters that they could move elk by using a chainsaw. They'd pack a chainsaw on their horse and get into an area and fire it up a few times. They'd run it for a while and then move on to another drainage and do it all over again. The noise would move elk out of one drainage and into another, hopefully the one that their hunters were working at the time. The same thing can be done by firing a rifle in a bedding area. Or talking too loudly on the trail. Or making any excessive, abnormal noise in elk country that will move elk out of there.

The whole key to making the most of elk movements like this is to know the area well enough that a hunter can be posted on the path of the escaping bulls or cows. This is the type of knowledge that doesn't come easily. It takes some map work, scouting, and, better yet, some visual experiences during the hunting season, to know which trails and passes the elk will use when they're pressured. Elk will often use a particular saddle to drop into the next drainage. They might work their way through a particular patch of timber. There might be a small open park that they usually cross.

Once you know where they're likely to go, it doesn't take much pressure to push the elk in that direction. Instead of the massive white-tailed deer drives that many visiting hunters are accustomed to, an elk drive can be pulled off by just a hunter or two.

One of the best examples was a hunting trip that I went on with Keith Wheat and Orvis Lovely. Wheat and I decided we were going to try to get Lovely an elk.

We knew about a drainage that had some bulls in it, but we didn't know how many. Our plan was to drop off Lovely in a good spot on the escape route and move the elk toward him. So Wheat and I circled the big basin, dropped into the timber, and hadn't been sneaking through the woods for more than a half-hour when we heard Lovely fire from his spot on the ridge nearly two miles away. When we finally got over to him, he explained that there were three bulls in the group and he had dropped the biggest, a five-point. The others, two young bulls, had dropped back into the timber.

With a wise, old bull, there's seldom any doubt as to what the animal will do. It will move out of the country. But young bulls are different. They make mistakes. And the two bulls that Lovely had spotted did just that. Wheat and I simply went in the direction where they had headed, made another swing through the timber, and Wheat jumped them, taking one of the young bulls with a single shot.

In that single drainage, two drivers and one hunter on stand had taken two bulls in what was really a single push through the timber. The key was knowing where the escape route would be and applying just enough pressure to get the bigger bull moving. The second bull was a bonus because we knew that younger bulls often don't react as strongly to the pressure and stay in an area that can be hazardous to their health.

As a hunter adds to the knowledge of his hunting area, he can probably apply the principles of making a push through the timber toward a hunter waiting on stand. Even if that hunter always takes to elk country alone, knowledge of the escape routes can help him when he gets into a situation where other hunters are moving the elk around.

You can do this, of course, without having to rely on a midnight ride into a national park. You can do it with a few other hunters in your own group or unwitting hunters you don't even know. Knowledge of the paths that elk will take when they're not pushed, and the escape routes that come into play when they are, is the type of information a hunter can rely on after he's been at the game for a while. And it's the type of experience that will often result in filling your tag, while those around you can only hope for a big stampede.

Have We Gone Too Far?

Few dreams burn as brightly in the mind of a western hunter today as the vision of a trophy bull elk square in the sights of his favorite hunting rifle. How many of these regal bulls are symbolically shot by hunters in the days and weeks that lead up to each elk season would be a matter of pure conjecture. But it's a sure bet that there are more of those dreams than there are trophy bulls in the whole length of the Rockies.

That dream, however, is nothing new. In the old days, it might have been a big dry cow that was lined up in an old buckhorn sight. It might be the spike or raghorn of a hunter's teenage years that a first-timer hopes for as he tries to bargain his way into a more manageable dream with God. Or it might be the trophy bull in a veteran's vision that is so large that it would put everything else in the Boone and Crockett Book to shame.

To reach those ends, hunters have tried many methods over the

ATTENTION ELK HUNTERS

Come to Gilbert's Hunting Lodge!

Located one & half miles southeast of Jardine in the heart of the best hunting country

We have warm bunk houses, comfortable beds (for 36 hunters), home cooked meals and good saddle horses.

OUR PRICES ARE AS FOLLOWS:

Board and Bed - $2.50 per day

Saddle Horse - - $2.00 per day

Elk packed and snaked in from $1.50 to $10
(according to distance)

*Write for prices on week-end fishing trips
and Hell Roaring hunting trips*

Gilbert's Hunting Lodge
JARDINE, MONTANA

The fees charged by outfitter Clyde Gilbert look like a real bargain compared to the fees of today. Don Laubach photo.

years. They've tried to put themselves in the best possible position to get an elk. And they've relied on the latest technology available to help them along.

One of the more interesting pieces of elk hunting lore that

illustrates the point is an old outfitter's handbill that's framed in the home of Gardiner outfitter Warren Johnson. The handbill was used to advertise the outfitting business of Clyde Gilbert, who began catering to hunters coming to the Gardiner area beginning back about 1920. Compared to today's prices, Gilbert's paycheck from hunters seems almost comical or tearful, depending on which end of the checkbook you happen to be located. Gilbert advertised, "ATTENTION ELK HUNTERS Come to Gilbert's Hunting Lodge! We have warm bunk houses, comfortable beds (for 36 hunters), home cooked meals, and good saddle horses. Our prices are as follows: Board and Bed—$2.50 per day. Saddle Horse—$2.00 per day. Elk packed and snaked in from $1.50 to $10 (according to distance)." In today's inflated market, those prices seem ridiculously low. But as one hunter put it, "You know, they still charge two-fifty per day, it's just the decimal point that has changed."

The thing that always interested me about the old handbill was that people were interested in improving their chances of getting an elk even back in the early days of this century. It's really no different today.

Just as Clyde Gilbert must have felt the pressure to find an elk for his clients, the outfitter of today has the same burden on his back to produce. And I fancy that even back then, there were hunters who felt such a strong obsession to bag an elk, that all forms of natural reason left them once they stepped into elk country. They must have rode poor Clyde unmercifully back then when days passed without seeing or shooting elk. They must have complained about his high prices. They must have been an almighty pain in his backside. And, as any outfitter of today will tell you, that hunter is still alive and well or, at least, hunters carrying the same mean and ornery genes still are very much a part of the business.

The question comes up in hunting circles as to what makes a person just a serious elk hunter and what makes a person obsessed with bagging an elk? At what point do you go too far in your search for a legal elk or a trophy elk? Where do you draw the line?

All we have to do is look around us to realize that the elk hunting game has changed a great deal since Gilbert was packing hunters into the backcountry. Man's technology has raced ahead while the animals we seek have basically stayed the same.

Clyde Gilbert, second from left in the black cowboy hat, shows off some of the elk taken by his hunters. Dick Herriford photo.

Some hunters, for example, are fond of saying that mule deer are stupid because they tend to run away for a distance, then stop and look back at the hunter before heading off over the hill. Yet this evolutionary trait was the very thing that kept mule deer alive in harsh climates over the centuries. In contrast to the skittish whitetails, mule deer would conserve their energy and make a positive identification of the source of danger before they burned up precious calories. That mode of defense worked fine against the wolf, coyote, black and grizzley bears, and even primitive man. Standing out there at three hundred yards and using keen eyesight to spot a Sioux, Crow, Blackfeet, or Cheyenne that was far out of bow range, served the mule deer well. He didn't run long distances to escape and burn all those calories unless he had to. It's only in the past century that the scales have been tipped in man's advantage because of long-reaching, exceptionally-accurate, high-powered rifles. Yet instead of marveling at the mule deer and the energy-efficient defenses he developed to survive over time, we smugly call him stupid.

In different ways, the advance of technology and man's settling of the West has also worked against elk. In Gilbert's day, a few hunters used horses and many more hunted on foot or on snowshoes to go after elk. Today, we have a vast array of additional devices to penetrate elk country in all seasons. We have four-wheel-drive trucks. We have human-powered mountain bikes. We have motor-powered trail bikes. We have three-wheelers and four-wheelers. We have cross-country skis and snowmobiles. And if you really want to see where the elk are hiding out, you can take to the air in helicopters and airplanes and scout entire drainages in minutes in search of the bull of your dreams.

Changes in the land itself have also worked against the elk. Logging roads and mining roads have opened up drainages to one-day hunting trips that used to require several days to pack into on horseback or on foot. Dense stands of timber that elk once used as hiding places to escape hunters have gone the way of the two-by-four, with logging leaving elk in those areas much more vulnerable to hunters than they were in the past. Recreational developments and subdivided cabin sites on the fringes of our mountains have gobbled up critical winter range. And the human presence in search of recreation in all seasons has put a new stress on animals trying their best to make it through a cold winter or to raise their young in the heat of summer.

If you look at our weaponry and other equipment, that too has changed. It's possible now to shoot a rifle with tailor-made ballistics to the job at hand. They'll shoot far and flat. Instead of the old buckhorns and peep sights, you can take aim with a scope sight that makes even the most distant animals look close. The days of the old long bows and cedar arrows are gone and archers rapidly moved beyond recurve bows to compounds with wheels and cables able to move an aluminum-shafted arrow through the air almost faster than the eye can see them. To spot game now, we have the benefit of fine lenses in our binoculars and spotting scopes. We use bull calls, cow calls, calf calls, elk scent, range-finders, and laser sights, just to make ourselves more efficient hunters.

Modern fabrics make clothes lighter and warmer. Alloy packframes make it possible for loads of elk meat on your back to weigh little more than the meat itself. There are light tents and sleeping bags that make a backcountry camp warm and comfortable. There are walkie-talkies and CB radios which hunters are

With all the modern methods at our disposal, at what point have we tipped the scales too much in our own favor in search of elk. Michael H. Francis photo.

using to coordinate activities as they move in for the kill. And there are books and videos that can make a hunter a relative expert at elk hunting before he even sees elk country through his own eyes.

Through all of these changes, the elk have remained basically the same.

At what point, then, does the hunter have an unfair advantage over the elk? Have we tipped the scales so badly in our own favor that we should step back and rewrite the rules of the game?

You'll get no definitive answer to that question here. In fact, it's impossible and probably not even desirable to take things back to the way they where during Clyde Gilbert's time.

There are some things going on, of course, that are pretty easy to decide one way or the other. It isn't right, for example, for a hunter to be up in the air spotting elk from a plane or helicopter early in the morning and be on the ground just hours later drawing a bead on those elk. When there are so many roads into an area that elk find it impossible to escape the influx of hunters, it's reasonable to close the road during the hunting season. And if every stitch of security cover for elk in an area is due to fall to the logger's saw, it's time to limit the logging before all the elk are shot into extinction.

But even in these situations, the call may be a difficult one and be based solely on a hunter's own personal prejudices. In the end, it may not be what is legislated against, but what we decide on our own, that dictates when we've gone too far in search of elk and we've stepped over the line. But that doesn't mean there won't be a need for some legislation and regulations to help the situation along.

Already, we have saturated the backcountry with hunters in many areas. When hunters have struck out so far from one side of the mountain that they're bumping into hunters coming in from the other side, there isn't any more wilderness in which the elk can hide. When we've shot up our bull population to the point that there aren't enough left to ensure decent production, we've harvested too many. And when the silence of elk country is replaced by the day-long drone of trail bikes, four-wheelers, snowmobiles, or four-wheel drives, we've taken away too much of the thing that brought us to elk country in the first place.

It's a testament to elk as a species that despite all the changes modern technology has brought to the places they live, elk are still a formidable adversary in the hunting game. An elk, whether it's a cow, spike, raghorn, or mature bull, is still an animal to be treasured and appreciated when a hunter is lucky enough to hang his tag on one.

But a hunter has to remember that just because the trophy is so great, that still doesn't justify taking that trophy by any means. Hunting that elk one-on-one on his home turf remains the most enjoyable aspect of the game. Doing your homework. Exploring the territory. Learning about the species. Making the most of the mountain experience. Executing the perfect stalk. Firing the one, well-placed round. All these things only enhance the elk that may be waiting for you at the end of your hunt.

As I said, you'll get no definitive answers here about whether or not we've gone too far. But I will say that if you rely too heavily on modern technology to be your ally and to do your hunting for you, you've only cheapened the challenge that elk hunting presents you. You've tarnished the trophy at the end of your hunt. And you've sold yourself short as a hunter in pursuit of the greatest game animal of all.

■

CHECKING YOUR OPTIONS

It's man's nature, I suppose, to fight against too much prosperity. After so much time and effort put into becoming a veteran elk hunter, the elk hunter begins to change the rules. If he finds too much success, he begins to make things tougher on himself. It's almost as if the elk hunter wants to be an underdog again in his quest for success.

To increase the challenge facing him, the elk hunter often opts to change weapons. The smokeless powder rifle with its flat trajectory and long-reaching bullet is exchanged for something else.

For an increasing number of hunters, the switch is to a weapon used more commonly more than a century ago. The move is on to black powder and some states have recognized the change and made special regulations to cater to this type of weaponry. Instead of long range shooting, the animal must be closer and it must be taken with the first shot. That's a new challenge for the elk hunter.

Others switch to handguns for their elk hunting and opt for shooting elk at even closer range. For the handgun hunter, like the black powder shooter, the skill level must also be great to stop an elk. It takes plenty of practice to use these short-barreled weapons and have them be as effective as the long guns.

Or, the elk hunter may switch to bowhunting. In many states, that opens up new calling opportunities because archery seasons often coincide with the rut for elk. This, too, is a short-range weapon situation. And with the chance that an elk may come roaring in to close range to take up the challenge of a bugle, the excitement factor alone may be enough to infuse some adrenaline into the veteran's hunting.

It's all variations on a theme for the elk hunter who has learned his lessons well and become consistently successful at putting meat in the freezer.

For the elk hunter, the trail ahead of him is much shorter now. And he wants to get all the enjoyment he can out of the rest of the way.

Burning Black Powder

I don't pretend to be an expert on hunting with a black powder rifle. All I know is what I've heard from other hunters and seen what my hunting companions have done with it. And to a man, they say it's unbeatable fun in elk country.

Hunting with black powder is both as old as our earliest predecessors on this continent and as new as the latest kit rifle being carried into the wilderness today. In fact, the move to black powder has been increasingly strong in recent years as more and more hunters have taken up these guns as their weapons of choice.

In some ways, the reasons hunters are turning to black powder is a matter of self-limitation. Hunters have mastered the smokeless stuff and the long-reaching guns that are able to strike out at three hundred and four hundred yards and stop an elk in its tracks. Now, they want to challenge themselves further by using a more traditional weapon throwing .45 or .50 or .54 caliber projectiles designed to effectively take elk at much shorter ranges.

To hunt with black powder successfully, a hunter generally has to get within a hundred yards of his prey, though some well-practiced hunters may try shots farther than that. The hunter generally won't take a running shot at an animal either, waiting instead for the more certain target that a standing or walking elk provides. And they need to be so well-versed in the way their weapon handles that they can take their game in a single shot because second shots are hard to come by.

Most hunters have to get within a hundred yards and kill an elk in a single shot to use black powder effectively. Bob Zellar photo.

In short, a black powder hunter has to know his own capabilities and the way his gun will handle long before he steps into the field. He has to learn those things on the practice range and be able to apply those lessons to hunting situations before the game gets too far away. It's only when those lessons are learned well that a black powder shooter can take aim at an elk with confidence.

For that reason, most black powder hunters step into the elk woods long after they've passed their novice tests at elk hunting with other weapons. By the time they burn black powder, they're experienced hunters already. But even if they have the experience, black powder has a way of humbling a person.

One friend of mine got his humbling when he drew a late season cow permit a few years back and decided to try to fill the tag with a .45 caliber Hawken. I knew where there were some elk holding in a bunch of quaking aspen, so I elected to go along and show him the way.

We had to hike about a mile in the pre-dawn darkness to reach the stand of aspens. Once we got there, we spotted two cows in the quakies right where we thought they would be, but they were still too far away. My friend and I dropped into a creek bottom and started to make a sneak on the elk, but the cows spotted us long before we were able to stalk within range. Those cows headed out and all we could do was drop back and plan a new strategy.

That strategy resulted in a long and fast loop around the elk, as we hoped to get in front of them and have another chance at the two cows. This time, our plan worked. The two cows came through the opening ahead of us at about a hundred yards. My friend took dead aim at one of them and squeezed off the trigger. As the Hawken filled the morning air with its cloud of smoke, my friend's .45 caliber bullet missed its mark. Had he been shooting a smokeless gun, he could have tried another shot. If he had missed again, he could have shot a third time before the two cows disappeared from view.

With a black powder gun, however, second shots are rare. That's just one of the limitations a hunter puts on himself. In order to shoot again, he has to pour more powder, place his patch and ball, trim the patch, ram it all home, and then prime his rifle with either more black powder or a percussion cap. By the time most hunters finish that reloading process, the elk have moved into the next drainage. There's no apologies for the time it takes to reload from the black powder elk hunter, it's just part of the game.

But at least one black powder elk hunter found the cow call to be an invaluable aid to getting an elk last year. That hunter was a fellow from Colorado who wrote to me that he had jumped some elk in timber but managed to sneak up on the bunch again, closing to within twenty yards. Whether it was an errant twig, a pine bough or just a simple miss, the elk took off after the hunter squeezed off his shot. The hunter said he started to cow call at

Black powder areas have been set aside in some states for hunters to use their primitive weapons in hunting elk. Wesley Brandon photo.

the elk immediately, while he worked to reload his rifle. By the time the gun was reloaded, one of the elk had wandered back to within twenty yards and this time the hunter didn't miss.

Another tale of a black powder shooter putting his cow calling skills to good use came from Washington. There was a hunter there who had forty-seven years of elk hunting experience heading into the field last fall. This time, the man and his partner heard a bull bugling from a ridge above them and began to make cow and calf sounds. The calling brought the bull down off the ridge and across two hundred fifty yards of open ground to give them a forty-yard shot.

The ability to call elk in close or to stop them for a second shot has added a new dimension to elk hunting for the black powder shooter. The ability to stop them for a standing shot is another benefit.

With or without the aid of cow calls, it's a fair bet that black powder shooting will gain in popularity in the years ahead. Some states have already set up special seasons available to black powder shooters. Other states have set aside certain hunting districts for their use. But even if no special considerations have been made for these hunters with primitive weapons, black powder shooting has enough going for it in its own right to ensure its success in the future.

The challenge it presents to the hunter makes it an exciting alternative to guns shooting smokeless powder. And the pride of a hunter who scores on a truly good bull with his black powder gun creates a traditional tie with the past and a sense of satisfaction that spans the centuries.

Back to the Bow

It's a special time when autumn first lays its hands on the high country. High mountain meadows feel the nip of the first frosts. Evening breezes blow sharp and cold as they sweep down the canyons. And the quaking aspens, those beautiful groves, see their leaves turn from green to gold.

It's time for the elk to brush the velvet from their newly-hardened antlers and to make their first tentative squeals echo through the high country. It's time for blue grouse families to begin their odd ascent from the valleys to the mountaintops to spend the winter high when everything else is low. And it's time for the bowhunter to don his camouflage of green and brown and gray and try to blend in with the autumn scene as best he can to better search for elk.

In much of elk country, bowmen get an early break in being the first hunters of the year to head for the high country. They feel the odd mixture of seasons that can have the morning dawn frosty cold, the mid-day sun bake the earth hard, and the evening breeze be cold enough again to force warm hats and gloves onto the bowhunter.

Of all the options available to the elk hunter looking for new challenges, bowhunting has probably attracted the majority of veterans seeking new ways to hunt elk. There are several reasons for this. For one thing, it's the time of year that a bowhunter heads into the mountains. The weather is beautiful. The backcountry is accessible. For another, mastering the equipment isn't as tough as it used to be. A person can learn to use a compound bow fitted with sights in a small fraction of the time it took to master a longbow or recurve without sights. And finally, it's the elk themselves. They're bugling during the bow season in most states and the prospect of calling a big bull in to close quarters is a thrilling thought indeed.

Of all the alternatives to rifle hunting, however, the bow is still perhaps the most demanding. Most successful bow shots on elk are taken at ranges of thirty-five yards or less. To make it a better shot, the elk should be within twenty yards. That's really close. A hunter has to know what he's doing to avoid spooking elk that are close enough to be able to read the brand name on his bow and arrows. He has to know the animals well enough, too, to put himself in position for such a shot. And he still has to log plenty of hours on the practice range to make sure his arrows will hit the mark. After all, it does get damn embarrassing to explain away misses on elk so close that you feel you could touch them with your bow.

Elk hunting with a bow also takes some restraint. Rifle hunters may take three hundred, four hundred, or even five hundred yard shots with the knowledge that if they only hit the elk, they stand a good chance of slowing it down enough that they can get him. But a bowhunter has to know that based on the results of his practice, an elk fifty yards away may still be out of range. He has to

Bowhunters increase the challenge by having to call elk to within close range to get a shot during archery seasons. John Potter photo.

know, too, about the bone structure that lies beneath the thick covering of hair and hide. Bullets will smash their way through to reach the vitals. Arrows do not. A bowhunter has to avoid shots in the shoulder, the shoulder blade, the neck, the head, or anywhere else that the mass of muscle or bone will keep the arrow from making a killing shot.

Making the decision not to shoot at an elk that would be so

ridiculously easy to harvest with a rifle is not always easy. Believe me.

A couple of years back, I was just two weeks out of the cast on a broken left ankle and out of the elastic support on a sprained right ankle when bow season arrived. I vowed to give it the best shot I could, even if my mobility was severely limited by the recent injuries.

I hobbled and wobbled down the trail for the first two days of the season with my partners, gentlemen to a fault, who slowed their own progress to stay with me. But by the third day of the season, I pressed upon them to go and hunt. They could go so much further and stand a much better chance of running into elk if they only left me behind. I'd just limp along in the places nearer to camp and honestly enjoy the freedom of autumn in the mountains after a housebound summer on crutches.

It really was enjoyable. I moved along slowly. I stopped to enjoy the sight of a cow and calf moose. And I took out my elk calls and made the music that all elk hunters can only play at in the weeks that lead up to the season. Finally, I reached a place where the trail dropped off in front of me into a deep basin. To the right and left were side slopes, the kind that mean pure agony to weak ankles. So as far as I was concerned, my hunt ended there.

I sat down with my back to a tree, ate a candy bar, and blew on my cow call for a while. Just for spice I added a squeal on the bull call. Then I cow called some more, squealed some more, and ate another candy bar. I honestly don't know how long I had been sitting there blowing on my calls when I heard the fateful crunch of something stepping on a twig behind me. Peeking back around the tree, I saw a four-point bull sneaking through the timber, looking my way. It came as a big surprise, seeing that bull starting to circle just thirty-five yards away.

As I nocked an arrow and pulled camo mesh down in front of my face, the bull kept walking slowly, keeping his distance. For the next five minutes or more, I talked to him with the cow call and kept his interest. But though I was sorely tempted several times, the bull never gave me the clear shot I was looking for. And eventually, the bull wandered back in the direction he came from, dropping back into the basin.

In my poor condition, it seemed a miracle that I could call an elk in. Not within a half-mile of camp. Not with these ankles. After

Hunters have to know a great deal more about the animals they seek to be able to hunt effectively with a bow and arrows. Mark Henckel photo.

the shakes subsided, I went back to having fun, blowing on my calls and enjoying the high mountain morning. After all, I'd had my thrill. But after another long period of calling, I heard another crunch behind me. Peeking around the tree again, I couldn't believe my eyes. This time, there was a different four-point bull there. And a four-by-five, too.

These elk had also come in slowly and silently. They were also walking a circling course thirty-five yards away. And these elk, too, seemed fascinated by the cow and calf sounds. But these elk didn't turn back. They kept circling until the lead bull, the four-by-five, finally stepped into a clearing and stopped. At thirty-five yards, after many minutes of waiting and watching, this bull finally presented the clear shot I was looking for. And the arrow I sent after him ended up burying itself to the fletching, taking out his lungs, and giving me a bowhunting trophy in a year that seemed sure to be one without an elk to show for my archery efforts.

In retrospect, the interesting thing about the elk that day are the many lessons that they taught about bowhunting, hunting with calls, and hunting in general.

Unconsciously, I had put myself in a position where the elk were

Bowhunters rely on extensive use of camouflage to hide themselves from the sharp eyes of an elk. Frank R. Martin photo.

somewhere below me and I was calling them up the slope. Elk seem to far prefer to come up to a caller above them rather than to come down the slope to one below them. The reason may be one of safety on the elk's part. If they come up, they know they can flee much more quickly downhill on their backtrail than they could if they have to run uphill to get away from danger.

As far as bowhunting is concerned, it reinforced the fact that there's just no excuse for taking a bad shot. Had I not overcome the desire to shoot at the first elk, I never would have had the perfect chance at the other bulls. Had I shot at the first bull, I might have missed him and spooked him out of the country. Or I could have made a poor hit that would have resulted in a lost elk. In either event, the decision to shoot at the first bull could easily have been disastrous when compared to the way the hunt turned out.

Checking Your Options

And finally, it showed me that there's no substitute for patience in waiting out an elk. In this case, the patience was a forced condition. Had my ankles been solid beneath me, I never would have stayed in that spot for so long. I'd have been a mile away before that first bull had the urge to come in. But by being patient and working the call, the elk had eventually become interested enough to come in. They had come in quietly. They had come in slowly. But they had come in. It made me wonder how many other chances I had blown because I hadn't been so patient and had moved off too quickly.

It's also interesting to point out that the elk of this story were taken in the weeks before the rut. In those three days of hunting, none of our hunting party heard a single bugle. That makes me wonder whether the same scenario might have been worked out other times had I been more patient during the rifle season in the weeks after the rut.

It's these kind of close encounters with elk that make bowhunting such an interesting option for hunters. In most cases, the hunter comes out of these encounters with his elk tag still firmly implanted in his pocket. But there are often more close-range thrills in bowhunting, even when you don't shoot an elk, than you can find in a lifetime of rifle hunting.

For that reason, you can expect more veteran hunters to decide to give bowhunting a try in years to come. Compared to the old recurve or longbows that were so hard to shoot at even forty-five or fifty pounds of pull, they'll discover that sixty-five or even seventy-five pounds of pull in a compound bow that fits their draw length is relatively easy to shoot. The reason is that after reaching peak weight the wheels break over and the hunters are holding back only about half that amount when they take aim at the target. It's no wonder why many hunters opt for eighty or ninety pounds of pull in their elk bows.

But anyone who chooses to give bowhunting a try should realize that his equipment and archery license are just his ticket into the game. The real enjoyment comes from the glorious weather of early autumn, the chance to see the seasons change in the high country, and the thrills that close encouters with elk seem to provide every time.

Even with the help of today's bull and cow calls and the rutting time for elk to help you along, there are still no guarantees that a bowhunter will bag an elk. But he is just about guaranteed to have the time of his hunting life trying for an elk with a bow.

Packing a Pistol

There's a certain freedom to walking elk country without a rifle or bow in your hands. You can move easier, pick things up with both hands, and feel more like you're taking an autumn stroll than taking part in a serious elk hunt. But if you see an elk, you can reach to your hip, draw your handgun, and still have something to hang your tag on and put in the freezer for the long winter ahead.

Few hunters start out in their pursuit of elk packing a pistol. Most are rifle hunters, or even bowhunters, who hunt that way for many years before deciding to add a new dimension to the elk hunting game by trying to take one with a handgun.

That, at least, is the way I got started. I had gone through the entire spectrum of rifle hunting and had even hunted with a bow in the early 1950s. For the bulk of my years, however, it was the long-reaching rifle that put elk meat in my freezer. In fact, it almost grew to be a sure thing. If I did my scouting, spent enough days in the field, and worked hard enough at it, an elk was all but guaranteed.

My move to the pistol was to put a little extra challenge into the elk season. It would limit me to shorter-range shooting and that would demand more of me as a hunter. Besides, I had taken a black bear earlier that year with my Thompson Contender. It would be nice to add an elk to the list of that handgun's accomplishments.

There was a problem to be overcome and I frankly underestimated it at the time. The biggest barrel I had for the Contender was a .222. That might be a fine caliber for varmints or even a well-placed shot on a deer or antelope. But it was definitely light for elk hunting. Still, it was the best I had and I was bound to make it work for me. If I could only have a good, clean shot with the Contender and have a steady aim with the 1.5-power scope, I knew I could get the job done.

I was hunting with Mark Wright that year. He carried a rifle. I carried the pistol. So at least I had someone to back me up if things went really sour. We decided to hunt down a snowy ridge

Deep snow played a role in helping to stop an elk that was taken with a handgun some years ago. Michael H. Francis photo.

and had been moving along steadily for about two hours when we spotted a bull across a canyon. The range was much too far for me, but it looked like a good shot for Wright. As I watched through my binoculars, he took aim and fired. I could see that the shot hit the elk, but I didn't know where, and we watched together as the bull ran off through the deep snow into the timber.

As we were crossing the canyon to follow up the shot, I looked through the binoculars again and spotted a second bull that was moving through the timber above where the first bull had been. Now, there were two elk up there.

After scouting the area where Wright had hit his bull, we started along the blood trail and soon found that the two elk had met and begun traveling together. This called for some strategy on our part, because both bulls seemed to be going strong and it looked like they could get away from us easily. The tactic we chose was a time-tested one that has helped many an elk hunter score in years past.

I would hunt about a hundred yards behind Wright and about a hundred yards above him on the side slope. That way, if any elk tried to circle around him, the bull would probably bump right into me. In that arrangement, we started moving along the slope slowly, watching ahead for any sign of the elk. At some point along the way, however, I lost track of Wright. In fact, I didn't know exactly where he was until I heard him fire a single shot up ahead of me.

It was shortly thereafter that I saw a six-point bull coming back my way on a course that would take him to a point about fifty yards up the slope from me. I stood my ground and took a firm rest on a tree with my pistol. When the elk stopped about fifty yards away, I fired. But the elk didn't move. So I fired again. Again the elk didn't move. I stood there dumbfounded until I finally saw his head drop.

In piecing the story together later, I realized that my first shot had been a good one, right through the vitals. That shot must have startled him. The second shot hit the elk right next to the first. By that time, the bullets were doing their work and the combination of deep snow and the deadfall in front of the elk turned out to be a formidable enough barrier that the bull couldn't leap or walk around it to escape.

I learned later, when Wright told me, that both bulls had been together when he jumped them. He had finished his elk off with that single shot. And the other elk had come my way, giving me the close-range target that I needed. Both were full-antlered six-points.

It was a seven-mile walk back to where we had left the vehicle. We got there at about dark. The next day, we loaded up some horses and went back in to pack the elk out. It took four horses and the better part of that day to pack out all the meat.

Since that six-point fell to my .222, I've improved my elk arsenal. I've graduated into a .30 Herrett that's a much better caliber for the job of downing an elk. But it certainly isn't the only caliber that can down a bull.

Many hunters have used a .357, .38, .44, or .45 with success.

It takes plenty of practice and the right caliber handgun for a hunter to expect success in his search for a bull. Michael H. Francis photo.

These are probably the most popular loads that handgun hunters are using today. They may be the most popular in the years to come. But with so many wildcat loads being developed like the .30 Herrett, a hunter would do well to keep his mind open for the possibility of upgrading the elk-downing ability of his handgun.

Just as in black powder shooting, the important things a handgun hunter has to keep in mind are that he must know his weapon well and must be patient in waiting for the right shot. There are some shooters today, especially those who excel in the handgun silhouette game, who can reach out a fair distance and down an elk. Their guns are set up to shoot at distances of a hundred yards or more. But they also practice long-range shooting on a regular basis.

For most of us, a fifty-yard shot is much more makeable, even if the target is as big as the ribcage of an elk. Even then, it's going to take plenty of hours on the practice range to make such a shot a sure thing.

The benefits of handgun hunting for elk come in the form of the reward for being able to hunt this way. You don't have to drag a seven or eight or nine-pound rifle up the mountain with you. You put more pressure on yourself to make a closer stalk or to plan a better ambush. You have to know more about the animals themselves and the country they live in if you're to beat the odds.

But when it's all done, you've got a prize that you can truly be proud of. When you get your bull with a handgun, you'll have accomplished something that few other hunters even try. And you'll have taken the prize with a short barrel that so many hunters with a long barrel have yet to achieve.

■

END OF THE HUNT

Just as any trail has a beginning, it must have an ending too. And so it is for the elk hunter.

But what do you do when you reach the end of the trail? Do you just sit there and bask in the fact that now you know it all? Or do you realize, as you sit there, that there are other trails that still need to be explored?

Do you hang up your gun and leave the elk hunting to the youngsters still learning the things that you know? Or do you help them along and speed their passage?

For every elk hunter that reaches the end of the trail, the answer will be different. Just as all hunters take slightly different routes, they all react to the finality of the end in slightly different ways. But for all of us, the end must come in some way.

All we can hope for is someone to make the end of the trail a happier place. We can hope that there are hunters coming down the trail that have the same sense of wonder over the things that they learn, and the same feeling of reverence for the elk which so richly deserve it.

As you walk the trail of the elk hunter, realize that we all are truly blessed to be able to share, for a time, the world that the elk call their home. We are among the chosen few that have been lucky enough to spend our energies in a place and time so rich and full of nature's beauty.

If we only reach the end of the trail with the same sense of humility that we learned early in our development as an elk hunter, then perhaps we will be able to provide wise counsel to those who come behind us. If we only remember that the elk are made up of much more than meat and bone and hide, then maybe we'll begin to know what the game was all about.

In every elk hunter that walks the full length of the trail, there is the spirit of the hunter and the spirit of the elk forever entwined. And that's the way it always should be.

So Now You Know It All

I met a man once who knew all the things there were to know about elk and elk hunting. At least, that's what he told me. It was after one of my elk calling seminars that he came up to the front of the room and told me so. He didn't need to read any books. He didn't need to watch any videos. He didn't need to read any newspaper or magazine articles. And he didn't need to talk to anyone about it, including me. He had the elk and how to hunt for them all figured out, even if he didn't fill his tag last year.

All I could tell the man was that I was happy for him and wished him well. And I told him my own story. I said, "I've hunted elk all my life and I still don't know it all. And I probably never will."

Had the man stuck around longer, I would have added that I hope I never do learn all there is to know about elk and elk hunting. That's one of the things that keeps me going back to the mountains in all seasons every year, to be with the elk once again and to see what I can learn of their secrets.

As I said early on in this book, the whole experience of the game of elk hunting is like a big puzzle. When we're new at the game, we're not even sure what the puzzle is supposed to look like. But as we mature in our hunting and immerse ourself in all the resources of books, articles, videos, and personal contacts with other elk hunters, we begin to pick up pieces. As we mature as an elk hunter ourselves, we start putting those pieces together. And by the time we become a veteran elk hunter who can consistently find success at the game, our puzzle progresses toward

The hunter who thinks he knows it all will be in for some surprises each time he heads into elk country. Bob Zellar photo.

a fairly complete picture.

But one of the best parts about elk and elk hunting is that the picture is never really complete. There are new problems we can add to the hunting part of the puzzle, throwing in variations like black powder, bows and arrows, and handguns. Those new problems are complicated enough that they can keep us working at the puzzle for many more years trying to solve it. Yet even if those variations are solved, there's the unknown of the elk themselves that will always keep us going.

Because we can't physically communicate with the elk, we'll never really know all there is to know about the animal. We can make some insights, like where they happen to be at a particular time of year. We can define their physical needs of food, clean water and air, and a place to live. We can play with their ears with an elk call or befuddle their noses with elk scent. But the basic communication gap caused by the fact we can't ask questions of them and have them answer us means that we'll never know all the nuances of being an elk or how the life of an elk is changing over time.

Perhaps the most frustrating thing for the person who has paid his dues, put in his time, and has become a master elk hunter over the course of his lifetime is that all he's really learned by all this is that now, he finally knows what questions need to be asked. But he knows full well, too, that the only way he can get the answers is by doing more of the same things in elk country that he's been doing all his life. He watches elk. He listens to elk. And he learns from other sources all he can learn about elk.

The fact that elk will always remain something of a mystery shouldn't detract from what we have learned about the animals, however. In recent years, we've made some great strides in working toward a more complete picture of elk. Through the use of radio transmitter collars, wildlife biologists have a better understanding today of where elk go, when they go there, and what they do once they get there, than ever before. There has been pioneering work about how elk relate to one another, how bonds are created by different herd segments, and about how vast and far-reaching elk country really is when it comes to how the animals use the land in which they live.

In hunting, there have been dramatic breakthroughs as well. It wasn't that long ago that the only elk sounds a hunter ever made was a three-note whistle of a bull during the rut. The use of cow talk and calf talk as a widespread hunting tactic is a product of this decade. That development has allowed rifle hunters of October, November, December, and beyond to have the same excitement of calling elk that only a few riflemen and bowhunters enjoyed in the past. The use of scents in general, and the spray misting strategy in particular, has also opened up new avenues for hunters in all seasons. And the simple fact that there's popular literature and video cassettes to help the hunter to learn about these things, instead of tactics being hoarded only by the few, has created an opportunity for even those who live far away from elk country to increase their odds of success when they embark on the hunt of a lifetime.

To predict what the new breakthroughs will be in the years ahead would be difficult indeed. Throughout time, the bulk of

The more we learn about elk, the more we are just learning what question to ask to truly understand them. Michael H. Francis photo.

the consistently successful elk hunters have relied on the most modern weapons, equipment, and tactics available at the time. Each of those hunters also believed that the art of elk hunting had progressed as far as it would go. Yet who could have envisioned today's flat-shooting, far-reaching rifles a century ago when they were using black powder? What bowman with a longbow or recurve could have imagined that a complete archery survey of today would have discovered the fact that nearly nine out of ten bowmen in one state were using compound bows? And what hunter on horseback in the old days would have believed that gas-powered vehicles could carry hunters into the far reaches of elk country in hours when it took him days to reach the same spot long ago?

End of The Hunt ■

The only sure bet is to say with conviction that we're in for more changes in the years ahead. The elk will change. The elk hunter will change, too. But that's not necessarily bad.

Nearly all the changes that have been adopted over time by hunters have been embraced because they made the hunter more proficient in his pursuit of elk. They made it easier to reach the elk, see the elk, stalk the elk, or hit the elk. To me, that's progress well worth learning about.

My reason for wanting elk hunters to be more proficient at the game of elk hunting is for the elk themselves. It will always be possible for fish and game departments to limit the elk kill in their states by applying special and more restrictive regulations. What they have more trouble limiting is the wounding, the hunters out there who don't know what they're doing, the animals that die but are never found, and the hunter who takes the iffy shot instead of waiting for the sure shot that will make the sure kill.

This book has tried to present a picture of what elk hunting was like in the past, in part to preserve some of elk hunting's history and also to show how things have changed over the years. Some of that past was romantic, to be sure. But you can't escape the fact that elk were often treated with far less reverence by hunters in the old days than they are today. To many, they were simply meat on the hoof to be harvested in any way possible. The firing lines and elk slaughters and the single hunter who shot and shot until all elk were on the ground wouldn't be tolerated by most of today's elk hunters. Yet he was not only tolerated, but encouraged to do it that way by nearly all other hunters years ago.

Today's elk hunters are more likely to understand that a big six-point bull is a creature to be revered and the chance to hunt for him and perhaps hang a tag on him may very well be a once-in-a-lifetime experience. They're more likely to know about the hardships of winter, the perils of a dry summer, and the stress created in areas where there are too many hunters and too little cover in fall for the elk to hide. By learning about elk and elk hunting, these hunters' puzzles are more complete than at any other time in elk hunting's past.

For the years that a six-point bull has escaped the bullets and arrows and harsh weather, this elk deserves our respect. For the chance in this day and age to hunt for him and explore the wild places, elk hunters need to give thanks. And for the opportunity

Different hunters age differently and some continue to hunt for elk well into their seventies and beyond. Mark Henckel photo.

for elk and those who love them to share the same space and time in all seasons, we should learn all we can about the animals and how to hunt them.

We owe it to the elk to be as proficient and humane in harvesting them as we can. To do that, we should all make it our business to spend as much time as we can learning as much as we can about elk and elk hunting.

No matter what people might tell you, we'll never know it all.

The Hunt Goes On

Even elk hunters grow old. That may come as a shock to you, but it's the truth. It's also the truth that in many ways, elk hunting is a young man's game.

Now before the gray hair starts standing up on the back of some necks, it should also be pointed out that all elk hunters do not get old at the same rate. Some elk hunters grow old at forty. Others may be old at sixty or seventy or eighty. Yet surprisingly, still other elk hunters have been known to be young in their elk hunting at age ninety-plus.

What we're talking about here is the age when a hunter finally says he's had enough of elk hunting. It's time he turned in his elk hunters' union badge and drifted off to the golf course. He's leaving the elk to younger hands.

It's not a topic that is dealt with very often in outdoor literature. In fact, most things written on the outdoors would lead you to believe, in a twist of the old saying about death, that old hunters never hang up their guns, they just die. Yet it's a fact of life in many outdoor pursuits that there's a definite end to playing the game. It's especially true that there's an end to elk hunting for many veteran elk hunters. The most popular way to say that things have come to an end is something like, "I could care less if I ever shoot another elk. I've taken my share."

The simple truth about elk hunting is that if you do it right and play the game hard, elk hunting is hard work. As we get older, we almost have the feeling that the trails we are walking have been imprinted on the land by nothing more than our own bootsteps. It gets tougher to keep the muscles in tone between seasons and our bones and joints seem more susceptible to the aches and pains that come in the sometimes harsh weather of

Our aims often change as we get older and our reasons for being in elk country change with them. Mark Henckel photo.

autumn.

As we listen to our bodies talking to us, many decide not to punish themselves the way they did in earlier years. The drive to get to the top of the mountain isn't as strong. The deep snow seems a more logical barrier than it was before. And in some ways, the challenge of hanging a tag on an elk seems less important.

For some veteran hunters, the saying that they've taken their share of elk is undoubtedly true. When they were in their younger years, when there were families to be fed and the meat itself was more important, they very likely did shoot their share. They more readily accepted the work that was part of elk hunting as well.

Anyone who has handled even a few elk and has hunted them for more than a season or two knows that to be consistently successful, a hunter has to work at it. There are scouting trips to be made. There are pre-dawn, stumbling hikes toward distant parks and meadows on trails lit only by starlight. There are horrendous deadfall jungles that must be traversed. And once you get the elk on the ground, the work really starts. Even with a horse,

End of The Hunt ■

the lifting and tugging and packing demands muscle. Without a horse, you're almost always in for a long bout with liniment when the job is done.

Is it any wonder that a round of golf sounds more appealing than a hike to the mountaintops? Why should it be a surprise when the veteran changes strategy and decides that going low and slow is the better way for him to hunt.

There should be no stigma to this kind of decision. It shouldn't deserve sidelong glances or crude comments that the hunter has finally gone over the hill. It should be taken for what it is, and that's a change in direction for the veteran hunter.

Some older hunters keep their inner fires burning and their desire to keep hunting is still ablaze well into their sixties, seventies, and beyond. They somehow manage to keep themselves in good enough shape to play the elk hunting game and keep up with the kids. But many more simply transfer their energies into new directions.

Many of these hunters become more concerned with the elk themselves than the elk hunting. They put their energies into being conservationists, protecting what's left of their hunting world for the generations that come along behind them.

You may find them packing a camera instead of a gun. The pictures they take in all seasons will be treasured every bit as much as the elk that hung from the meat pole in their younger years. And even if no one other than their immediate family see the pictures they take, these photographic memories become a new cause for great joy.

You may find that they're more likely to be teaching and helping younger hunters get their elk than they are shooting elk themselves. If they still pack a gun, they may end up passing up shots they'd never have let get past them in earlier years. But now, it's more important for the youngsters or the hunters who have never shot an elk to do the shooting. If the veteran does pull the trigger, it will be only at the biggest of bulls or the choicest of elk for eating, depending on his particular desires at the time.

A hunter's perspective changes. The challenge has left us and, as a result, we put new restrictions on ourself and make the challenge harder. Or, we resign ourself to hunting after the migration when the animals are on the winter range. Those hunts are less punishing on the body. And if we can't meet the new challenge

Many hunters who hang up their guns will look to photography instead as they continue to learn about elk. Michael H. Francis photo.

or the winter range hunting goes sour, we simply come home empty-handed with no harm done.

As likely as not, the veteran hunter who says he has had enough will rediscover some other pastimes that were put aside for elk hunting years ago. Summer scouting trips will be replaced by a new zeal for fishing. Early season hunting will give way to a time-worn shotgun and a stroll for upland birds. And the coming of winter with the late elk season will be the time for smoking whitefish or doing a little ice fishing.

At some point in time for the veteran hunter, the ego trip of shooting that elk every year drifts away. It isn't such a big thing anymore to go out and shoot an elk.

In a way, the change in the veteran is a refreshing one. Rather than a time of sadness for times gone by, it should be viewed as a time of fulfillment. It's a new beginning for many hunters that removes all the demands for success and puts the veteran back in the field with new eyes and a new perspective on the game.

The veteran hunter knows that with him, or without him, the hunt goes on. The welfare of those elk he has grown to love is still his primary concern whether he's part of that hunt or not. And if he chooses to hunt hard for the elk or simply partake of

End of The Hunt ∎

bits and pieces of the elk hunting experience, he's at peace with himself. He can do whatever he wants.

By the time a person comes of age as an old elk hunter, he really feels he has taken his share. The pressure is off. And it's all just for fun now.

Next Year and Beyond

Whenever I walk among elk, in the pristine lands they call home, I wonder what it will be like when I can go there no longer. It's a morbid thought. It's a time that I never really want to come. Yet it doesn't take too many years of elk hunting to realize that it has to come to an end sometime.

Elk live in the untamed lands left on this continent. They are a creature of the steep and the rugged and the deadfall. In most cases, they are the reward that comes at the end of a long, tough hunt. And, as they say so often, the real work starts when you get one on the ground.

In the prime of our lives, that elk hunting equation means that we get into a little better shape, hunt a little longer, and work a little harder to hang our tags on a good animal. But as our bodies age, it gets to be a losing battle with time.

There are some hunters who tend to age better than others. I've known some who still chase elk into the seventies and eighties, and even a few in their nineties that head into the field each fall with a renewed vigor. But that isn't most of us. And even for them, there will be a last trip sometime.

The question then is what will happen to us, with our wealth of knowledge on elk hunting and the ingredients that lead to elk hunting success? I'll admit I really don't know. But my fondest dream is to live a day like the one I had late last season with a man I hadn't seen in years.

The story began in the pre-dawn gloom when I walked over to the Town Cafe to have a morning cup of coffee. Most of the hunters had gotten there ahead of me and were devouring their last forkfuls of eggs and hashbrowns and toast as I walked in the door. I sat down next to an older man, ordered a cup of coffee, then glanced over at him.

I said, "Aren't you Bus Lahren?" He said, "Yes."

It turned out that the man had hunted deer years before in the

The old hunter thought it might be the last elk of this life and he wanted to make sure he did it right. Don Laubach photo.

same part of the Crazy Mountains that my relatives had. He knew my uncles and my dad. I knew his boy. I asked him what he was doing in town and he explained that he had come up to do some hunting, having drawn a cow permit for the late elk season. A friend was supposed to go with him, but didn't show up. So seventy-five-year-old Bus had decided to go by himself. I explained that I would be happy to take him out, but couldn't that day. If he was still there the next day, however, I'd go out with him. I mentioned that I'd meet him at the same place, same time, and we'd leave from there.

The next morning came and I walked into the restaurant and there he was, ready to go. We sat and talked over coffee for quite a while, trading old stories. And when hunting time drew closer, I walked back home, fired up my four-wheel-drive pickup, and climbed into hunting clothes. As we waited for the truck to warm up, I asked him about his hunting and the things he had done. He told me that he used to hunt a lot on horseback and would carry a scoop shovel on the back of the horse so that when the horse got in deep snow, he could shovel it out and put on chains.

I knew right then and there it was going to be a good day. My elderly companion may have some years on him, but they hadn't dimmed the twinkle in his eye or dulled his sense of humor. It was a very good sign. This hunt wouldn't have the seriousness of the hunts of long ago when we were bound to come home with something. In this case, if we got something that was fine. If we didn't, that was fine too. It was a day for jokes and fellowship and reacquainting the old man with an elk world he first met long ago.

The time of year was perfect for our situation. Elk were already down and concentrated on the winter range. That would make for relatively easy hunting for my friend. And the old man himself looked to be a living testament to elk hunting. Better than most, he showed that once elk hunting gets in your blood, it's pretty hard to boil it out. There was a twinkle in his eyes and a spring to his step as he loaded his gun and pack and got ready to head down the road.

Bus was shooting an old Winchester .30-06 that he had bought in 1946. He paid $200 for it with a scope on it. Back in those days, that was a lot of money. And it still was in mint condition, despite the fact that the scabbard that held it showed the signs of the many horses it had been packed on.

As we drove toward the hunting area, I told him we'd try not to climb too many hills and would hit the easier spots first. At the first spot we stopped, we got lucky. There, before us, were about fifteen head of elk out in the sagebrush at about a hundred-and-fifty yards away. When I pulled the truck off the road, I situated it so he could use the hood of the vehicle for a rest. As my old friend settled in to shoot, the elk stood up and started to move, and I blew on the cow call to stop them.

But Bus was having trouble. After seventy-five years, his eyesight was starting to fail him. As the elk started moving up the hill, he was having trouble picking out a cow among the calves and bulls. Finally, he picked out a cow and I verified it and he shot. And missed. And shot. And missed again. And the elk went over the hill.

As we drove on to find another bunch of elk, Bus was upset with himself. He figured this could likely be the last chance at an elk he'd have in his life. And he had missed not once, but twice. As an elk hunter, he knew what that meant. He knew chances like that didn't come along often and it was no time to be flinging lead aimlessly. The old man wanted to pick his shot and make it, not just for himself, but out of respect for the animals he was shooting at and the elk hunting game he had played well all his life.

As luck would have it, we spotted a second bunch of elk down the road a little way that started moving through the timber at about a hundred yards. So Bus got ready again. But again his eyes failed him. With the elk weaving through the trees, he couldn't pick one out. This bunch, too, got away.

The old man laughed at himself and shook his head at this point. He told me he was having a great time. He enjoyed hunting with me. But now he had let two bunches of elk get away. His chances of getting the last elk of his lifetime could hardly be worse.

As we rolled down the backroads of elk country, I tried to console him. I told him we'd run into some other elk. And, if we didn't, that was the game of elk hunting. It was a fact he knew well.

Driving along, we talked of elk calibers and crosshairs in the scope and the country itself. We told tales of how we hunted and where we hunted. It turned out, we were very much the same despite our difference in years. We had walked the same places and worked the same strategies, though Bus was doing it as an adult in the years when I was still a child. He kept telling me, "Kid, you know this country. You're the guide. You just take me where you want to go." But if the truth were really known, the old man probably knew as much or more about the country than I did. He had hunted those mountains twice as long as I had. But

End of The Hunt ■

The things a hunter learns in elk country go far beyond just the knowledge it takes to tag an elk. Michael H. Francis photo.

he was just happy to have someone go along and help him in his search for an elk. And, the man knew what he was after.

We had seen some good bulls and he commented about them. But he was an old-timer that knew what he shot was what he was going to eat. He didn't want an old bull or a young calf. He wanted a cow that would give him the best chance for both plenty of meat and good eating.

Our casual conversation was enough to put the hunt on an even keel again. The missed elk were gone from his mind and the jokes began once more. As we drove through a patch of trees, I told him to stop looking down the slope. With me to do the dragging, I wasn't about to let him shoot something downhill from the truck. It was elk uphill from us, or nothing at all, and we both laughed.

And when I rounded the next corner, I looked downhill and there were two cows bedded down. Uphill drag or not, by that time I would have done anything for this man to help him get an elk. So I told him to get ready to shoot.

Driving past where the elk were, I stopped the truck and we quietly walked back. The two elk we saw bedded down turned into a bunch of seven when they stood up. Once again, I blew the cow call to stop them. And once again, Bus brought the old .30-06 to his shoulder. This time, there was no rest for him to use and the old gent knew it. "I can't hold this tning still," he told me. "And with this wind, my eyes are watering." It was only a hundred and twenty-five yards, but under the conditions, it was a tough shot. Picking out the biggest cow, Bus touched off a round and the elk crumpled with a clean shot through the lungs.

We tagged and dressed the elk, then the old man gave me an old but firm hand in the dragging of the animal back up to the road. For being seventy-five, the man had quite a pull to him. I had volunteered to cut the elk in two for him to make handling it easier. But he said no, if we could get that elk out whole, he'd rather have it that way. We used two ropes thrown over a tree branch and the truck to hang the elk. The truck pulled the elk up with one rope. I tied off the other. Then I drove under the cow and we lowered it neatly into the bed of the pickup.

As we drove off, the old man was obviously happy. It certainly wasn't the toughest elk of his life. It wasn't the biggest trophy. But it looked good to him and it came at a time of life when an elk alive or dead was probably appreciated more than it would have been in his earlier years.

We laughed all the way back to town. We had enjoyed a fine day together. But when we got back to the cafe, Bus figured he had to do something for me. "Well, what can I get you. I've got to buy you dinner or pay you or something. I just don't feel right about this," the old elk hunter said.

I'm afraid I laughed at him. I told him I wasn't taking anything. In truth, I felt it was something of an honor to be able to take him out and enjoy that day with him and I told him so. I said I just hoped that somebody would do the same for me when I got to be his age.

But Bus was still insistent, even when I started to head home. He said there had to be something he could do for me.

End of The Hunt ■

As each of us grows older, we only hope that those coming up behind us also appreciate elk and the country they lived in. Ron Shade photo.

Walking away, I stopped for a moment, turned, and finally said to my old friend, "I'll tell you what you can do for me. When I get to be seventy-five, then you can take me out elk hunting."

End of The Hunt